MYplace

FOR BIBLE STUDY

Published by First Place for Health
Galveston, Texas, USA
www.firstplaceforhealth.com
Printed in the USA
© 2018 First Place for Health

Cover design by Faceout Studio, Tim Green
Interior text design by Faceout Studio, Amanda Kreutzer

Unless otherwise indicated, all Scripture quotations are taken from The Holy Bible, *New International Version®, NIV®*. Copyright © 1973, 1978, 1984 by Biblica, Inc.® Used by permission. All rights reserved worldwide.

Scripture quotations marked KJV taken from the Authorized King James Version.

Scripture quotations marked MSG taken from *The Message*. Copyright © 1993, 1994, 1995, 1996, 2000, 2001, 2002. Used by permission of NavPress Publishing Group.

Scripture quotations marked NLT are taken from the *Holy Bible, New Living Translation*, copyright © 1996, 2004, 2007 by Tyndale House Foundation. Used by permission of Tyndale House Publishers, Inc., Carol Stream, Illinois 60188. All rights reserved.

Scripture quotations marked RSV are taken from the Revised Standard Version of the Bible, copyright © 1946, 1952, and 1971 the Division of Christian Education of the National Council of the Churches of Christ in the United States of America. Used by permission. All rights reserved.

© 2018 First Place for Health
All rights reserved

ISBN: 978-1-942425-27-4

CONTENTS

MY PLACE FOR BIBLE STUDY: BOOK ONE

Forever Changed

Foreword by Vicki Heath 4
About the Author 5
About the Contributors 5
Introduction 6
Week One: The Power of the Mind 8
Week Two: What's God Like? 30
Week Three: Prayer: Conversing with God 54
Week Four: Reframing Obedience 76
Week Five: What Does God Think About Me? 98
Week Six: Moving from Fear to Freedom 120
Week Seven: Keeping First Things First. 144
Week Eight: When Life Is Hard 166
Week Nine: It's Not All About Me. 192
Week Ten: Forgiveness: What It Is, What It Is Not 216
Week Eleven: Review and Reflect 238
Week Twelve: Time to Celebrate!. 239

Additional Resources
Leader Discussion Guide 240
Jump Start Menu Plan 252
Steps for Spiritual Growth 272
God's Word for Your Life 272
Establishing a Quiet Time 275
Sharing Your Faith 279
Endnotes 282
First Place for Health Member Survey 285
Personal Weight and Measurement Record 287
Weekly Prayer Partner Forms 289
100-Mile Club 309
Live It Trackers 311
Scripture Memory Verses 335

FOREWORD

I was introduced to First Place for Health in 1993 by my mother-in-law, who had great concern for the welfare of her grandchildren. I was overweight and overwrought! God used that first Bible study to start me on my journey to health, wellness, and a life of balance.

Our desire at First Place for Health is for you to begin that same journey. We want you to experience the freedom that comes from an intimate relationship with Jesus Christ and witness His love for you through reading your Bible and through prayer. To this end, we have designed each day's study (which will take about fifteen to twenty minutes to complete) to help you discover the deep truths of the Bible. Also included is a weekly Bible memory verse to help you hide God's Word in your heart. As you start focusing on these truths, God will begin a great work in you.

At the beginning of Jesus's ministry, when He was teaching from the book of Isaiah, He said to the people, "The Spirit of the Lord is on me, because he has anointed me to preach good news to the poor. He has sent me to proclaim freedom for the prisoners and recovery of sight for the blind, to release the oppressed, to proclaim the year of the Lord's favor" (Luke 4:18-19). Jesus came to set us free—whether that is from the chains of compulsivity, addiction, gluttony, overeating, undereating, or just plain unbelief. It is our prayer that He will bring freedom to your heart so you may experience abundant life.

God bless you as you begin this exciting journey toward a life of liberty.

Vicki Heath, First Place for Health National Director

ABOUT THE AUTHOR

Grace Fox is a popular Bible teacher and national co-director of International Messengers Canada. Together with her husband, Gene, she trains and leads short-term mission teams to Eastern Europe annually. Her ministry includes training church leaders in the Middle East and Nepal. She. has written nine books, including *Moving From Fear to Freedom: A Woman's Guide to Peace in Every Situation*, and she is an annual contributor to the Guidepost devotional *Mornings with Jesus*. Grace lives on a sailboat in Vancouver, British Columbia. She and Gene have been married for thirty-seven years and have three married children and seven grandchildren. Visit www.gracefox.com and www.fb.com/gracefox.author.

ABOUT THE CONTRIBUTORS

Lisa Lewis, who provided the menus and recipes in this study, is the author of *Healthy Happy Cooking* and *Deliciously Happy*. Lisa's cooking skills have been a part of First Place for Health wellness weeks and other events for many years. She provided recipes for twelve of the First Place for Health Bible studies and is a contributing author in *Better Together* and *Healthy Holiday Living*. She partners with community networks, including the Real Food Project, to bring healthy cooking classes to underserved areas. She is dedicated to bringing people together around the dinner table with healthy, delicious meals that are easy to prepare. Lisa lives in Galveston and is married to John. They have three children: Tal, Hunter, and Harper. Visit www.healthyhappycook.com for more delicious inspiration.

Christin Ditchfield Lazo, provided the spoken word recordings of Scriptures and Scripture-based prayers embodied in the Forever Changed digital download included with this study. Christin Ditchfield is a professional educator, author, conference speaker, and syndicated radio host, passionate about calling believers to a deeper life of faith. For nearly twenty years, she hosted her own radio program, Take It To Heart!® heard daily on stations across the country and around the world. She has written more than 70 books, including a number of Bible studies for First Place for Health. Christin holds a master's degree in Biblical Theology. For more information, visit her website at www.ChristinDitchfield.com. Original music by André Lefebvre, used by permission (www.barefootheartmusic.com).

Introduction

First Place for Health is a Christ-centered health program that emphasizes balance in the physical, mental, emotional, and spiritual areas of life. The First Place for Health program is meant to be a daily process. As we learn to keep Christ first in our lives, we will find that He is the One who satisfies our hunger and our every need.

This Bible study is designed to be used in conjunction with the First Place for Health program but can be beneficial for anyone interested in obtaining a balanced lifestyle. The Bible study has been created in a seven-day format, with the last two days reserved for reflection on the material studied. Keep in mind that the ultimate goal of studying the Bible is not only for knowledge but also for application and a changed life. Don't feel anxious if you can't seem to find the correct answer. Many times, the Word will speak differently to different people, depending on where they are in their walk with God and the season of life they are experiencing. Be prepared to discuss with your fellow First Place for Health members what you learned that week through your study.

There are some additional components included with this study that will be helpful as you pursue the goal of giving Christ first place in every area of your life:

- **Leader Discussion Guide:** This discussion guide is provided to help the First Place for Health leader guide a group through this Bible study. It includes ideas for facilitating a First Place for Health class discussion for each week of the Bible study.

- **Jump Start Menus and Recipes:** There are seven days of meals, and all are interchangeable. Each day totals 1,300 to 1,400 calories. Instructions are given for those who need more calories.

- **First Place for Health Member Survey:** Fill this out and bring it to your first meeting. This information will help your leader know your interests and talents.

- **Personal Weight and Measurement Record:** Use this form to keep a record of your weight loss. Record any loss or gain on the chart after the weigh-in at each week's meeting.

- **Weekly Prayer Partner Forms:** Fill out this form before class and place it into a basket during the class meeting. After class, you will draw out a prayer request form, and this will be your prayer partner for the week. Try to call or email the person sometime before the next class meeting to encourage that person.

- **Live It Trackers:** Your Live It Tracker is to be completed at home and turned in to your leader at your weekly First Place for Health meeting. The Tracker is designed to help you practice mindfulness and stay accountable with regard to your eating and exercise habits.

- **Let's Count Our Miles!** A worthy goal we encourage is for you to complete 100 miles of exercise during your twelve weeks in First Place for Health. There are many activities listed on pages 309-310 that count toward your goal of 100 miles. When you complete a mile of activity, mark off the box listed on the Hundred Mile Club chart located on the inside of the back cover.

- **Scripture Memory Cards:** These cards have been designed so you can use them while exercising. It is suggested that you punch a hole in the upper left corner and place the cards on a ring. You may want to take the cards in the car or to work so that you can practice each week's Scripture memory verse throughout the day.

- **Inspirational Download:** Each Bible study includes an inspirational compilation of spoken word, motivation for the journey or music available as a digital download. Look for the Dropcard inside your study with instructions about how to get your download.

WEEK ONE: THE POWER OF THE MIND

SCRIPTURE MEMORY VERSE
Love the Lord your God with all your heart and with all your soul and with all your mind and with all your strength.

Mark 12:30

Author John Ortberg writes, "The way you think creates your attitudes; the way you think shapes your emotions; the way you think governs your behavior; the way you think deeply influences your immune system and vulnerability to illness. Everything about you flows out of the way you think."[1]

My friend Maude proved these words true. She had been widowed in her thirties and had raised her kids alone on a financial shoestring. Now a stooped, gray-haired granny, she paid her bills by cleaning other people's houses. But Maude never complained. She wore a smile a mile wide, and her humble presence lit up the room. What was her secret to knowing contentment and joy? She had trained her mind to focus on all things good.

Our thoughts are foundational to who we are and who we hope to become. They impact our attitudes, emotions, and behaviors from the moment we open our eyes in the morning to the minute we fall asleep at night. If we want to become the people God created us to be and experience life as He intended, it is essential for us to develop godly thinking patterns. This happens as we allow God to renew our minds, which is what this study is about.

There is no single Greek word in the New Testament that parallels our English word mind, but two words used are frequently. The first word, *dianoia*, means "thinking through" or "thinking over" something. It also refers to the understanding that comes from that reflection. The second word, *nous*, refers to the "seat of understanding" and the "place of knowing and reasoning." It is regarded as the center of a person's ethical nature.

Sometimes, the matters we think through have little bearing on the big picture of our lives: I think I'll take a long walk today. It's been a while since I connected with so-and-so. I think I'll do the laundry later this week rather than today. Other matters we think through bear life-altering consequences: I think I'll marry this person. It's time for a new career—I think I'll quit my job and go back to school. I think I'll get involved in a First Place for Health group.

That's right—you read the last sentence correctly. If you are in a First Place for Health Group, you have realized your need to improve your health. You've pondered the time and financial commitment and considered the lifestyle changes you need to adopt. Kudos to you! This is an example of a "thinking over" that can alter your life forever for the good.

This session can be a significant stepping stone to the positive and permanent change you desire. You will identify several areas of your life commonly impacted by mistaken thinking and learn how to reframe or replace those thoughts with God's truth. When your mind aligns with His truth, you will experience true freedom—which is the destiny He desires for everyone.

— DAY 1: OUR MIND'S IMPORTANCE

Dear Father, please help me regard my mind as a gift to be cherished and nurtured. Help me understand the vital role it plays in who I am and hope to be. Amen.

The thoughts we habitually entertain determine the direction of our lives. This is great if we follow Maude's example and focus on all things good. But what if our thoughts frequently include comparison, criticism, fear, and lies?

Wrong thoughts left unaddressed can wreak havoc on every part of our being. Emotionally, they fill us with shame and convince us we're not "good enough." They influence the way we treat other people and determine whether we forgive or fall into bitterness.

Physically, wrong thoughts pave the road to ill health. Some cause anorexia or bulimia. Others tell us food fills our heart's deepest longings, or we can eat whatever we want whenever we want, or that we're too busy to exercise.

I speak from painful firsthand experience. Faulty thinking resulted in my losing mobility for three months after suffering a ruptured Achilles tendon and a knee injury. Both injuries were preventable had I developed correct thought patterns about my health.

Spiritually, wrong thoughts lead us down the same path Eve took when she doubted God's goodness and wisdom. They dupe us into believing it's okay to make up our own rules in lieu of God's commands. Worst case scenario, they separate us eternally from the one true God who created us for intimacy with Him.

Someone once said, "Watch your thoughts, for they become words. Watch your words, for they become actions. Watch your actions, for they become habits. Watch your habits, for they become character. Watch your character, for it becomes your destiny." It's true! Our thoughts determine our destiny, so ensuring a healthy mind is of utmost importance.

Satan knows this reality, so he attacks our minds. Read Genesis 3:1–7. What seeds of doubt did he sow in Eve's mind?

___

What thoughts went through Eve's mind? How did they influence her behavior (see verse 6)?

___

What was the outcome? How might her thought process and this outcome have changed if she had loved God with all her mind?

_____

_____

_____

_____

Recall an instance when you faced a frustrating or faith-testing situation. What thoughts did you entertain? How did those thoughts influence your attitude, behavior, and the outcome?

_____

_____

_____

_____

_____

What are your reasons for joining a First Place for Health group? List them here.

_____

_____

_____

_____

Satan will try to undermine your efforts to improve your health. He will plant lies in your mind: *You'll never be able to lose weight. You don't have time to exercise. You can eat whatever you want; it won't matter.* What lies is he already whispering to you?

_____

_____

_____

_____

_____

_____

You love God with your mind when you intentionally focus on His truth rather than the lies. Read Deuteronomy 20:1–4; Psalm 18:28–36; and Romans 8:31–32, 37. Which reference speaks to you the most within the context of your fitness journey? Why?

_____

_____

_____

_____

_____

> *God, help me love You as You deserve to be loved—with all my heart, soul, mind, and strength. Amen.*

— DAY 2: BE TRANSFORMED, NOT CONFORMED

Dear God, help me to understand the relationship between my mind and my ability to live a holy life. Amen.

The mind plays a key role in your personal transformation. Read Romans 12:1–2. One of the apostle Paul's reasons for writing this letter was to instruct believers in practical Christian living. In verse 2, he told believers not to be _____ any longer to the world's patterns of behavior. In order to accurately understand what this means, look up the word *conform* in a dictionary and write the most suitable definition below.

_____

_____

_____

According to *Webster's New World Dictionary and Thesaurus*, to *conform* means "to make similar; to be in agreement; to act in accordance with rules, customs, etc."[2] When we apply this definition to the verse, we know Paul wanted believers in Rome to refuse to fit into their unbelieving society's mold. They were to behave differently from the cultural norm and not be influenced by the crowd.

Paul may as well have addressed this manuscript to us! Studies show our culture has become obsessed with two things: how we look and what we eat. Spending brain power on how we look or what we want to eat next is a common worldly pattern of thinking. As believers, we need to resist these cultural behaviors as we strive to love the Lord with our whole mind.

First Peter 1:14–16 gives further instruction about not conforming. What does it say? Make this personal—what are three evil desires with which you struggle?

_____

_____

_____

To what standard of behavior does God want you to aim (see verse 13)? Why?

_____

_____

_____

Achieving a standard of holiness in everything you do sounds impossible. But when God issues a command, He will always give you the ability to succeed through His power. What are three actions that can help you resist being conformed to the shape of your wrong desires (see verse 13)? Practically speaking, how can you prepare your mind to resist temptation?

_____

_____

_____

Return to Romans 12:2. Rather than copy unbelievers' behavior, the believers in Rome were to be_____. Look up the word *transform* in a thesaurus and list appropriate synonyms below.

_____

_____

_____

One synonym for *transform* is *reconstruct*. This fits with the original Greek term that denotes *transformed* as meaning "to make essential and permanent changes." One commentary says *transformation* means we undergo change at the core of who we are. In essence, then, Paul is saying we are to become new people—totally altered, overhauled, reconstructed.

Compare this verse with 2 Corinthians 3:18. It's not wrong to think about how you look when you keep it in the right perspective. Into whose likeness are you, as Christ's follower, being changed? How does this truth encourage you today in your wellness journey?

_____

_____

_____

_____

So, what's the key to being transformed—made completely new on the inside?

_____

_____

_____

_____

In what areas of your life have you conformed to your own wrong desires or to ungodly behaviors on which society stamps its approval? What is one action you can take to renew your mind and begin making essential and permanent changes?

_____

_____

_____

Thank You, Father. Show me ways in which I can renew my mind so I can resist conforming to the world's standards. Amen.

— DAY 3: WHO'S IN CONTROL?

Heavenly Father, help me to understand what it means for the Holy Spirit to control my mind. I surrender it to You—change it and fill it with thoughts that bring a smile to Your face. Amen.

Read Romans 8:5–8. The apostle Paul divides people into two groups: those controlled by their sinful nature and those controlled by the Holy Spirit. Read the following verses and describe those whose minds are controlled by the sinful nature:

VERSE:	
Psalm 64:5–8	
Isaiah 32:6–7	
Philippians 3:18–19	
Romans 1:28–32	

In Romans 8:6, Paul says the mind of sinful man is _____ . In verse 7, he says it is _____ . Why can it not please God?

_____

_____

_____

This news sounds grim, but there's hope! Because of what Jesus did for you through His death on the cross, evil does not have to control you or determine your destiny. If you place your faith in Christ for salvation from sin and its consequences, the Holy Spirit comes to live in you. When He is in control, your mind is _____ and _____ (verse 6).

Still, life being what it is, your mind engages in a battle between good and evil in the process of your becoming more like Christ. It's not unusual for negative, critical, fearful, lustful, or self-centered thoughts to appear, sometimes at the most unexpected times. What types of thoughts sometimes pop into your mind?

_____

_____

_____

_____

How often do thoughts about food come to mind? How would you describe their influence over your behaviors?

_____

_____

_____

_____

Your role is to refuse to entertain faulty thoughts. Besides asking God for help, what specific actions can you take to overcome them?

_____

_____

_____

_____

Sometimes you will wrestle with memories of painful experiences either inflicted on you by others or by choices you made. Perhaps you failed to meet expectations at work, or you suffered a broken relationship. Wouldn't it be nice if your mind contained a delete button? One click, and *presto*—gone forever. Too bad life's not like that. So, what can you do? Read Philippians 3:13–14. The word *forgetting* isn't literal here; it means "refusing to dwell on." You refuse to dwell on, or "camp" on, painful memories. Why is this important?

_____

_____

_____

_____

Instead of focusing on the past, its pain, and those things you cannot change, you put your energy into what lies ahead. As Paul says, you press on toward the goal to win the prize for which God has called you heavenward in Christ Jesus. Paul also says what types of thoughts on which you should train your mind to think. Read Philippians 4:8. In the left column below, write the descriptive words Paul uses. In the right column, write their opposites.

PAUL'S WORDS:	OPPOSITES:

Identify one negative thought that recurs in your life. Look at the list of words above and circle the one that best describes it. Then write a short prayer below, asking God to change your mind and to help you develop the opposite, positive quality in regard to that thought.

_____

_____

_____

_____

Father, thank You for the Holy Spirit, who will make me more than a conqueror in the battle for my mind. Amen.

— DAY 4: THE MIND OF CHRIST

Dear Father, please give me a willing heart to fully cooperate with You, holding back nothing from Your Holy Spirit as He renews my mind and teaches me new spiritual truths. Amen.

A beloved old hymn offers this prayer: "May the mind of Christ, my Savior, live in me from day to day, by His love and pow'r controlling all I do and say."[3] In 1 Corinthians 2:16, Paul says, "'Who can know what the Lord is thinking? Who can give him counsel?' But we can understand these things, for we have the mind of Christ" (NLT). Read 1 Corinthians 2:11–14. What, or who, gives you the privilege of having the mind of Christ? Who does not have this privilege? How do they regard spiritual truths?

_____

_____

_____

Isaiah 55:7 says, "Let the wicked forsake their ways and the unrighteous their thoughts." What thoughts would an unbeliever initially need to forsake to receive the mind of Christ?

_____

_____

_____

When we place our faith in Jesus Christ for salvation, He sends His Spirit to live in us—to guide, comfort, convict, and teach us spiritual truths to bring about necessary and permanent change. He transforms our minds by removing our self-centered way of thinking and aligning our thoughts with God's thoughts. This is an ongoing process, just as the process of our being transformed into Christ's image is ongoing.

The more we mature in our relationship with God, the more quickly we recognize when our thoughts are contrary to God's and the more readily we make needed adjustments. Read 1 Corinthians 13:11. How might your thoughts about God and His ways resemble a child's reasoning? What should happen to those thought processes as you grow in your faith?

_____

_____

_____

Isaiah 55:8–9 indicates the need for our thoughts to be aligned with God's thoughts. Whose thoughts are higher? Whose thoughts are wiser? Explain.

_____

_____

_____

_____

Recall a situation in which you questioned this scripture. How did it prove true?

_____

_____

_____

Compare your thoughts to God's thoughts when facing the following situations:

SITUATION:	YOUR THOUGHTS:	GOD'S THOUGHTS:
Facing financial uncertainty		
Feeling inadequate		
Feeling afraid for loved ones' well-being		
Feeling rejected		
Feeling out of control with your eating		

Write a short prayer inviting the Holy Spirit to control your mind and bring your thoughts into alignment with His regarding a current situation you face.

_____

_____

_____

_____

_____

Lord, I confess that Your ways and thoughts are higher than mine. Develop Your mind in me so I'll view life through Your eyes. Amen.

— DAY 5: GUARD YOUR MIND

Father, thank You for peace that guards my mind and heart. This peace is a gift, and I humbly acknowledge You as the giver. Amen.

My husband and I lead ministry teams to Eastern Europe every summer. We've toured ancient castles perched atop high peaks. From that vantage, soldiers could see enemy armies approach from miles away. Rulers built these ancient castles with high walls to protect their residents from enemy attacks, and soldiers manned the gates day and night. No one entered or exited without the guards' approval.

Apply that imagery to Philippians 4:7—"And the _____ of God, which transcends all understanding, will _____ your hearts and your minds in Christ Jesus." Paul uses the military term *guard* to help us understand the role God's peace plays in our lives. God's peace—if we allow it to do so—acts like a sentry that protects our hearts and minds from thoughts that pose a risk to our well-being. It stands at the gate, forbidding entrance to Satan and his attempts to destroy us with weapons including worry, fear, jealousy, lust, greed, and anger. What thoughts are threatening your mind and emotions within the context of your wellness journey?

_____

_____

_____

_____

_____

WEEK ONE THE POWER OF THE MIND

Draw a circle. Inside the circle, write the words "my heart and mind." Outside the circle, write a few words that describe the thoughts you identified in the previous question. Now draw an arrow pointing to the circle itself and label it "God's peace."

The peace God promises is impenetrable to enemy attacks. The word *transcends* used to describe it implies something that far outshines anything else of its kind. The original Greek word suggests it is first-rate, first-class, and top-notch. We might seek peace from other means, but nothing even comes close to the peace God supplies. What an amazing gift!

God often prefaces a promise with a command. In this context, supernatural peace encompasses us when we fulfill our part. Read Philippians 4:6. Write this verse below and circle two actions you are to take. Now underline the attitude you are to demonstrate.

_____

_____

_____

Why is thanksgiving so important when you are in a crisis situation?

_____

_____

_____

MYplace O BIBLE STUDY

For what can you give thanks when everything seems to go wrong?

_____

_____

_____

Recall a difficult situation in which you intentionally gave thanks. How did doing so influence your overall attitude toward your circumstances?

_____

_____

_____

In Philippians 4:5, Paul offers another reason for peace. He says, "The Lord is _____." Compare this verse with Isaiah 43:1–2. How should this reassurance affect your perspective when you're afraid, confused, feeling crushed by sorrow or disappointment, or at a loss?

_____

_____

_____

How does this promise resonate with you right now?

_____

_____

_____

Dear God, help me to commit my concerns to You with thanksgiving so I can experience Your wonderful peace no matter what. Amen.

— DAY 6: REFLECTION AND APPLICATION

Heavenly Father, thank You for caring deeply about my well-being. Thank You for instructing me through Your Word and the Holy Spirit. Grant me a teachable heart to learn well. Amen.

Six weeks—that's how long I had known Gene Fox when he proposed. Thoroughly smitten, I said yes, despite the fact I knew next to nothing about him. We married six months later.

Decades later, I can practically read his mind. Gift buying is easy, because I know his preferences. I can predict what menu item he will order in a restaurant. I know what makes him sad or happy and how he'll respond in any given situation. I know his passions, his dreams, and what one thing he would change about his life if he could. I can even finish his sentences.

Understanding another person's thought processes to that degree doesn't just happen. It develops through spending time together, conversing, and listening to each other. It grows by walking side by side through life's thick and thin and sharing mutual experiences and values.

In the spiritual realm, we grow in our understanding of the mind of Christ by spending time in His presence and studying His words and life as recorded in the Bible. The more we understand who He is and what He did on our behalf, the more we grow in our love for Him. As our love for Him deepens, so does our trust in His goodness. And with that comes increased desire to submit to His authority in our lives.

The ultimate goal is for our minds to be completely transformed. This happens when we say no to the influence of our sinful natures and yes to the Holy Spirit's control. When He assumes authority over our minds, He identifies the uglies we have allowed to reside there. He teaches us how to deal with them and replaces them with attitudes Christ embodied.

In the King James Version, Philippians 2:5 reads, "Let this mind be in you, which was also in Christ Jesus." That's the goal for this study—for our minds to be renewed to become more like Christ's mind. As this transformation takes place, our behaviors also change to reflect His heart and values.

Take a few minutes to ponder your thought patterns in the following areas of life. What changes, if any, need to take place so they better align with Christ's mind?

My relationships

_____

My money matters

_____

My moral purity

_____

My eating habits

_____

My exercise habits

_____

My words

_____

My willingness to obey Him

_____

In your prayer journal, write a prayer inviting the Holy Spirit to transform your mind into the mind of Christ. Ask Him to identify faulty thinking patterns and to replace them with truth.

> Lord God, there is no other like You. You are blameless in every way. Please renew my mind, washing it from every impure and ungodly thought. Give me the mind of Christ, I pray. Amen.

— DAY 7: REFLECTION AND APPLICATION

Dear Lord, I'm grateful that when You tell me to be transformed by the renewing of my mind, You don't expect me to figure it out on my own. You command, and then You equip. Amen.

Annie attended the women's Sunday school class I taught. She joined discussions and knew all the right answers, but she didn't apply the truth of God's Word to her life. Heroin held her captive, and she spiraled down, down, down in every area of her life. Ultimately, the petty crimes she committed to buy the drug caught up with her, and she landed in a jail far from home. In her own words, it was the best thing that ever happened to her.

I scarcely recognized Annie when she reappeared several months later. Her complexion, once covered in sores, now glowed. Her frame, once skeletal, now looked healthy. Articulate words replaced slurred speech. Best of all, her conversation wasn't steeped in lies to mask her lifestyle. Instead, it bore witness to Jesus Christ and the work He was doing in her heart and mind. More than a decade has passed, and Annie continues to thrive. To this day, she's passionate about Christ and grateful He set her free and made her into a new person.

Annie's story resembles that of the apostle Paul. He, too, knew all the right answers to every theological question, but he didn't apply truth to his life until he met Truth personified (see Acts 9:1–9). His encounter with Jesus on the road to Damascus changed everything. And rightfully so. After all, Jesus proclaimed Himself to be the way, the truth, and the life (see John 14:6). He came to set the captive free, did He not?

Years after his conversion, Paul wrote a letter of instruction to the believers in Ephesus in which he said, "You must no longer live as the Gentiles do, in the futility of their thinking. They are darkened in their understanding and separated from the life of God because of the ignorance that is in them due to the hardening of their hearts" (Ephesians 4:17–18).

Paul wrote from experience because he, too, had formerly based his life on wrong thinking. He knew what life apart from God looked like, and he knew God had better things in store for these people. He encouraged believers to put off their old selves "being corrupted by its deceitful desires" and instructed them to "be made new in the attitude of your minds" and to "put on the new self" (Ephesians 4:22–24). He then gave specific instructions about how the new self would behave after their minds were renewed.

Paul's words hold true today. Let us not allow futile thinking to rob us of the life God intends for us. Rather, let's allow Him to change our minds and, hence, change our lives.

Heavenly Father, You make all things new. Make my mind new today. Change my thoughts and change my life to bring glory to Your precious name. Amen.

WEEK ONE THE POWER OF THE MIND

WEEK TWO: WHAT'S GOD LIKE?

SCRIPTURE MEMORY VERSE
No one is like you, O Lord; you are great, and your name is mighty in power. Who should not revere you, O King of the nations? This is your due.

Jeremiah 10:6–7

A.W. Tozer is recognized as one of the most influential American evangelists of the twentieth century. In *The Knowledge of the Holy*, he wrote, "What comes into our minds when we think about God is the most important thing about us."[1]

This quote has profoundly changed my life. I used to think the most important thing about us as believers was our legacy. Yet while legacy matters, I now understand that it—and everything else about us—flows from our thoughts about who God is. For instance, if we picture God as a divine authoritarian wielding a stick, we'll constantly be on heightened alert, watching our backs lest we do something wrong. We'll strive for perfection, hoping to please Him but always feeling we don't measure up. We'll struggle with the feeling of not being good enough and being unworthy of His love. We'll likely ask for forgiveness again and again for the same sin because we subconsciously doubt His willingness to wipe our slate clean. Our worship is fear-driven and not motivated by gratitude for all He has done for us.

If, however, we view God as a heavenly father who's crazy in love with us, we'll feel comfortable telling Him about everything that concerns us. We won't be afraid to admit when we've done wrong, because we know He will forgive us time and time again. We'll find courage in trusting Him to provide for our needs. We'll enjoy an ever-deepening intimacy by spending time in His presence. The more assured we are of His acceptance, the greater our hope, inner freedom, contagious joy, and ability to love others as He loves us.

So, how do we develop right thinking about who God is? There are several ways. First, we discover what He is like through the marvels of His creation (see Romans 1:20). The vast universe declares His power. The intricacy of the human body declares His intelligence. Infinite species of flowers, trees, insects, animals, birds, and sea creatures reveal His attention to detail, His delight in beauty, and even His sense of humor.

Second, we develop an understanding of God through our experiences. We discover Him to be our source of peace when chaos swirls around us. We find Him to be our guide when He answers our prayers for direction. We learn He is our comforter when we grieve the loss of a loved one. And, finally, our understanding about God deepens when we study His Word. That is where we learn about His names, read about people's encounters with Him, and discover what He declared to be true about Himself.

But there's one more means of developing right thinking about God: by studying the person of Jesus Christ, God in the flesh. Let's begin this week's study by focusing on Him.

— DAY 1: JESUS—GOD IN PERSON

God, to think You took on human form to reveal Yourself to mankind leaves me breathless! Open my spiritual eyes and give me a glimpse of Your beauty as seen in Jesus Christ. Amen.

Understanding God's nature is a lifelong process. Part of growing in that knowledge involves unlearning wrong thoughts we have believed about Him. Our upbringing and experiences influence those beliefs. Our concept of God as a loving Father, for instance, can be skewed if we've never known the love of an earthly father. And because every religion portrays God in a unique light, our spiritual heritage, of course, contributes to our understanding.

The same was true for the Jews in Jesus' day. From generation to generation, they had been taught the Messiah would come soon. They expected Him to arrive in kingly fashion, as a mighty warrior who would conquer the Roman Empire once for all. With that image in mind, it's no wonder they rejected Jesus—a carpenter's son and itinerant preacher who spent time with the outcasts of society. How in the world could He be their promised redeemer?

The people's false expectations collided with reality when Jesus appeared, and they were forced to unlearn wrong thinking to embrace the right. Take a few moments to write down your thoughts about who God is. Do any of these thoughts need to be unlearned?

_____

_____

_____

_____

Read John 14:6–11. Jesus was God in human form. In verse 7, He made this profound statement: "If you really knew me, _____."
How did Phillip respond to this statement?

_____

_____

_____

Phillip had spent three years doing life with Jesus. He had watched Jesus heal the sick, cast out demons, and raise the dead. He had listened to Jesus' teaching and His discussions with religious leaders. Yet still he lacked in his spiritual comprehension. What does this say about our need to remain teachable even if we have grown up with a godly heritage?

_____

_____

_____

_____

What claim did Jesus make in verse 9?

_____

_____

_____

_____

With that claim in mind, read the following verses. What do you know to be true about God based on Christ's words and deeds?

VERSE:	JESUS' WORDS/DEEDS:	TRUTH ABOUT GOD:
Matthew 8:23-27		
Matthew 15:30-32		
Luke 14:1-5		
Luke 14:12-14		
Luke 15:8-10		
Luke 19:1-5		
Luke 24:7		

Understanding God's character will give you hope when facing personal struggles. This is true even within the context of battling food issues. For instance, knowing God's power calmed a raging storm assures you that He can bring your raging cravings for junk food under control. Knowing He healed the blind, lame, and mute gives you confidence that He can heal your body as well. Which of the above truths resonate most with you on your wellness journey? Why?

_____

_____

_____

_____

_____

_____

Dear God, You are amazing beyond words. Thank You for giving us a glimpse of who You are by becoming flesh and dwelling among us. Amen.

— DAY 2: GOD IS GOOD

Dear Father, thank You for giving words of instruction designed to make me flourish. Help me to listen and obey with full assurance that You have only my good in mind. Amen.

Have you ever heard someone say, "God is good!" after hearing a favorable answer to prayer? It's wonderful to rejoice at a positive outcome, but we need to remember God is good even when He allows circumstances to happen that we don't understand... and even when we suffer. God is good—all the time—because it's His nature.

In Exodus 33:19, God said to Moses, "I will cause all my _____ to pass in front of you, and I will proclaim my name, the Lord, in your presence.'" God fulfilled this promise in Exodus 34:5–7. What words did God use to describe His character?

_____

_____

_____

_____

_____

_____

A key to trusting God with every detail of your life is to have a correct understanding about His goodness. Satan knows this, which is why he skewed Eve's thoughts about this attribute. When she doubted God's goodness, it made it easy for her to disobey Him (see Genesis 3:1–10). After Adam and Eve sinned, what two negative emotions did they feel toward God (see verses 7, 10)?

_____

_____

_____

_____

_____

_____

Because God is good, every command He gives is meant for your good. Read Proverbs 3:1–10. Identify the commands below and state how they benefit you.

VERSE:	COMMAND:	BENEFIT:
1-2		
3-4		
5-6		
7-8		
9-10		

Read 1 Corinthians 6:19–20. What command does God give in regard to your body?

_____

_____

_____

How does this command demonstrate God's goodness toward you?

_____

_____

_____

I used to think of my body as my own. Now I consider it as God's temple, and I am its caretaker. This change in thinking motivates me to make wise food and exercise choices. It makes me think twice before reaching for unhealthy snacks in secret and prompts me to exercise. Obeying this command has transformed my body, improved the way I feel about myself, and given me a hope-filled future rather than one filled with dread about increasing physical limitations. How could obeying this command benefit you in your wellness journey?

_____

_____

_____

_____

_____

Sometimes you will experience pain inflicted by people whose intent toward you is not good. No doubt Joseph felt pain after his brothers sold him into slavery, his master's wife accused him of rape, and authorities imprisoned him. Psalm 105:18 says, "They bruised his feet with shackles, his neck was put in irons." Read Genesis 50:15–21. What was Joseph's response toward his brothers when they were reunited? What allowed him to treat them with goodness?

_____

_____

_____

_____

_____

_____

Read Romans 8:28. This verse reassures us that "in _____ things God works for the _____ of those who love him, who have been called according to his purpose. According to verse 29, one of those purposes is to be "_____ to the image of his Son." The process may be difficult, but becoming more like Jesus is indeed good! How might God be using a current hardship to work something good in you?

_____

_____

_____

Dear Lord, forgive me for doubting Your goodness toward me. Help me to understand Your nature. Develop goodness in me as I relate to others. Amen.

— DAY 3: GOD IS LOVE

Heavenly Father, You love unconditionally, selflessly, and sacrificially. Teach me how to love others as You love me. Amen.

Frederick Lehman credits a patient in an insane asylum for penning the third verse to his hymn "The Love of God." Lehman states he discovered the lyrics, which the patient had adapted from an eleventh-century Jewish poet, on the walls of the patient's room after he had died:

> *Could we with ink the ocean fill,*
> *And were the skies of parchment made,*
> *Were every stalk on earth a quill,*
> *And every man a scribe by trade;*
> *To write the love of God above*
> *Would drain the ocean dry;*
> *Nor could the scroll contain the whole,*
> *Though stretched from sky to sky.*[2]

These lyrics move my heart to gratitude and worship. Oh, that we, too, could possess such an intimate understanding of God's love for us. It would protect us from the pain we experience when we act on our doubts about His ways or intent toward us.

Right thinking about God's love comes from filling our minds with the truth. Read Psalm 57:10, Proverbs 3:11–12, Zephaniah 3:17, Romans 8:38–39, Ephesians 2:4–5, and 1 John 4:9–10. How does Scripture describe God's love? How does God reveal it?

_____

_____

_____

_____

Now read Ephesians 3:17–19. How does Paul describe God's love (see verse 19)?

_____

_____

_____

_____

Paul writes that when you develop right thinking about God's love, you are "filled to the _____ of all the _____ of God" (verse 19). How does this bring hope within the context of weight loss?

_____

_____

_____

_____

Read 1 John 4:11–12 and compare with Mark 12:30–31. How might a correct understanding of God's love help you to love Him as He deserves? How might it help you to love others? How might it help you love yourself?

_____

_____

_____

Read 1 John 4:16–18. What are your three greatest fears in regard to your wellness journey? How might a correct understanding of God's love lessen or completely overcome those fears?

_____

_____

_____

John 3:16 is perhaps the most well-known Bible verse that describes God's love. Write it here.

_____

_____

_____

How did God demonstrate His love for you? What amazing gift does He want to give you because He loves you so much? Have you responded to His love by choosing to trust Him for eternal salvation? If not, what is hindering you? If you have questions about how to trust and respond to God's love for you, your group leader would be happy to answer them.

> *Father, I'm humbled and forever grateful for Your love that surpasses understanding. Amen.*

— DAY 4: GOD IS HOLY

God, teach me what it means when Your Word says that You are holy, and help me understand how this applies to me. Amen.

R.C. Sproul writes, "The primary meaning of *holy* is 'separate.' It comes from an ancient word that meant, 'to cut,' or 'to separate.' When we find a garment or another piece of merchandise that is outstanding, that has a superior excellence, we use the expression that it is 'a cut above the rest.' . . . When the Bible calls God holy it means primarily that God is transcendentally separate. He is so far above and beyond us that He seems almost totally foreign to us."[3]

Read Isaiah 6:1–3. Notice the word holy is mentioned three times in a row in verse 3. Jewish liturgy taught that stating a matter twice indicated extreme importance. Mentioning it three times was akin to shouting from the rooftop, "Listen up! You must pay attention to this!" Given this, why is God's holiness mentioned three times?

_____

_____

_____

_____

In ancient times, a king's greatness was demonstrated by the length of the train of his robe. How does Isaiah describe the train of God's robe (see verse 1)? What does this indicate about God?

_____

_____

_____

_____

Seraphim are six-winged angels who worship God continuously. Why did they cover their faces (see Exodus 33:20)? Why did they cover their feet (see Exodus 3:5 and Joshua 5:15)?

_____

_____

_____

_____

_____

What do the seraphim's actions indicate about God?

_____

_____

_____

_____

We minimize God's supreme excellence when we choose to live contrary to His commands. Our behavior reveals faulty thinking—that we're a cut above Him and can live as we please. Such thinking only leads to problems because our wisdom and integrity falls far short of His. Have you minimized God's superior excellence? If so, what has been the result?

_____

_____

_____

_____

In Revelation 4:1–11, John records a scene that is similar in some ways to Isaiah's vision. What attribute is mentioned three times in verse 8?

_____

_____

_____

How is God's supremacy celebrated in heaven?

_____

_____

_____

Someday we will celebrate God's supremacy when we stand before His throne, but we can start in the here and now. How can you celebrate His excellence with your mind? With your body?

_____

_____

_____

_____

God, You alone are holy, holy, holy. You alone are worthy of praise. Remove from me any thought that minimizes Your supreme excellence. Amen.

— DAY 5: GOD IS MIGHTY

God almighty, You are strong when I am weak. Help me find courage in this truth when I face battles that are too big for me to handle. Amen.

God revealed His character to people through His names as mentioned in the Bible. One of His Hebrew names, found in Psalm 24:8, is *"Yahweh Izzuz ve-Gibbor,"* which means, "The LORD strong and mighty." Write this verse below and circle the phrase, "The LORD strong and mighty." According to this verse, where does God display His strength and might?

_____

_____

_____

_____

The battle stories in the Bible are a fascinating study into human nature. They expose our tendency toward wrong thinking when facing challenges, lead us into the truth about who God is, and reveal how He fights on our behalf. Read Exodus 14:9–31. What was the Israelites' reaction as the enemy approached (see verses 10–12)? What did this reflect about their understanding of God?

_____

_____

_____

_____

How did Moses respond (see verses 13–14)? What enabled him to respond this way?

How did God reveal His strength and might on the Israelites' behalf (see verses 19–22, 24–25, 27–28)? What was another outcome besides the victory (see verse 31)?

Read Judges 7:1–25. Gideon had gathered 30,000 warriors to fight the Midianites. What did his actions reflect about his understanding of God? What was God's response to Gideon's battle plan (see verses 2–3, 7)?

Ultimately, who won the battle (see verses 9, 22)? What was another outcome other than the victory (see verses 14–15)?

___

Read 2 Chronicles 20:1–30. King Jehoshaphat felt fear when he learned a vast army was coming to attack, but he refused to dwell on those fears. What did he do instead (see verses 3–12)?

___

What are some phrases in Jehoshaphat's prayer that reveal an intimate knowledge of God?

___

Who devised the plan and fought the battle (see verses 15, 17, 20, 22)?
What were some other outcomes besides the victory (see verses 27–30)?

___

___

___

___

Sometimes the weight loss battle you face will seem impossible to win because your natural tendency is to feel afraid. For example, food often brings false security, so you may fear what will happen to that security if you cut back on portion sizes. These fearful thoughts are not wrong, but what you do with them matters. King Jehoshaphat refused to entertain fear. What was the basis for his courage? How did his response impact others (see verses 17–18)?

___

___

___

___

What role did praise play in the Israelite's victory (see verses 17–22)?

___

___

___

___

___

MYplace ○ BIBLE STUDY

Recovering your health might feel like a huge battle. Satan will try to convince you it's hopeless, but don't believe him. The truth is that God has a strategy for your situation. He will help you fight, and He can bring you to victory. What three insights from the battle stories you studied resonate with you the most? Why?

_____

_____

_____

_____

_____

_____

_____

_____

_____

_____

_____

Almighty God, I cannot fight battles in my own wisdom or strength. Thank You for promising to fight on my behalf. Amen.

— DAY 6: REFLECTION AND APPLICATION

Father, my heart bows in worship before You. You are King of kings and Lord of lords. Use this truth to transform my mind and, ultimately, my life. Amen.

This week's lessons are like grains of sand in the Sahara Desert. They offer only a tiny glimpse into how vast God is. Yet even a wee peek of truth—when applied—can be enough for us to initiate change and move one step closer to being more like Jesus. Correct thinking about God impacts every part of who we are. For example, here is how a proper understanding of His love can affect us when we are facing difficult circumstances:

MIND

We do not exhaust ourselves trying to make sense of our situation or dwell on our fears. We are able to rest in the knowledge that God's love surrounds us like a shield and nothing can touch us without His permission.

SOUL

We experience peace. Anxiety doesn't fill us, spill onto those around us, or negatively impact our relationships. Our response conveys courage to others, and they might ask us to explain our calm demeanor in the midst of the storm.

BODY

We are not ruled by worry or fear, so they can neither deny us a good night's sleep nor drive us to seek comfort in food or alcohol.

SPIRIT

We understand God's love, which gives us the freedom to pour out our hearts to Him. We turn to His promises for comfort rather than numbing our pain through negative behaviors.

MYplace ○ BIBLE STUDY

Now it's your turn. Choose from God's goodness, holiness, mighty power, or select a trait that resonates most with you from the list in Day 1. Describe how a correct understanding of the character quality you have chosen affects you when you are either (1) facing a crisis, (2) facing a major decision, or (3) dealing with a difficult person.

MIND
....

SOUL
....

BODY
....

SPIRIT
....

Dear God, thank You for Your Holy Spirit, who teaches me the things I need to know. I need to know more accurately who You are and allow truth to rule my mind, body, soul, and spirit. Teach me, I pray. Amen.

— DAY 7: REFLECTION AND APPLICATION

Dear Father, my mind cannot fathom Your greatness. Give me a glimpse of Your glory, and I will never doubt You again. Amen.

David Jeremiah writes, "Much of contemporary Christianity makes God out to be our Best Friend. And He is—but He's so much more than that.... We don't need a convenient, compact God. We need the one who causes us to fall on our knees, who leaves us speechless, who makes our eyes shine with His fire and causes us to depart as changed persons. And we need that God every moment of every day.... We need to rediscover our awe of God."[4]

It was a dark and stormy night when the disciples rediscovered their awe of God. Waves pummeled and filled their boat, and death seemed imminent. Terror gripped the men, and they shook God incarnate awake. "Lord, save us!" they yelled. "We're going to drown!" (Matthew 8:25). Jesus responded by saying, "You of little faith, why are you so afraid?" (verse 26). He rebuked the winds and the waves, and it was completely calm. The disciples were amazed and asked, "What kind of man is this? Even the winds and the waves obey him!" (verse 27).

Perhaps you, like the disciples, have experienced a time when God calmed the storm in an astounding way. He answered your cries for help with a revelation of His power that left you amazed, hope-filled, and hungry for more of His presence. Or maybe you can relate to the psalmist who, in the stillness of night, marveled at the wonder of God's love: "When I consider your heavens, the work of your fingers, the moon and the stars, which you have set in place, what is man that you are mindful of him, the son of man that you care for him?" (Psalm 8:3–4).

God's mind-boggling magnificence deserves our wonder. The more we understand the truth about who He is and what He has done for us, the more awestruck we become. Awe and wonder lead to humility and to our giving God His rightful place on the throne of our lives. With respect and obedience comes His blessing. And who wouldn't want that?

Unfortunately, some do not. Read Matthew 13:54–58. In this story, we read how Jesus' teaching amazed the people in His hometown—but then they allowed their wrong thinking about Him to permeate their minds. They minimized who

Jesus was and fell into unbelief. What were two results of their wrong thinking (see verses 57-58)?

_____

_____

_____

May we learn from their mistake and never reduce God to someone our size. May our thoughts be filled with truth—and may that truth transform us. Finish this week by writing a prayer in your prayer journal. Invite the God of wonders to adjust your thinking about who He is and to reveal Himself to you in new ways. Then get ready for the faith adventure of a lifetime!

> *Heavenly Father, how great You are! Guard my mind from ever minimizing You. Grow my understanding of who You are and use that truth to change me and make me more like You. Help me understand You as my portion. Amen.*

WEEK TWO WHAT'S GOD LIKE?

WEEK THREE: PRAYER: CONVERSING WITH GOD

SCRIPTURE MEMORY VERSE
Do not be anxious about anything, but in every situation, by prayer and petition, with thanksgiving, present your requests to God.

                                                    Philippians 4:6

I was raised in a family that prayed before meals and at bedtime. I still remember the words I uttered nightly as a little girl while kneeling by my bed: "Now I lay me down to sleep. I pray the Lord my soul to keep. If I should die before I wake, I pray the Lord my soul to take. Bless Mommy and Daddy and Grandma and Grandpa. Amen." For me, prayer was a rote tradition. I prayed because it was what my family did, not because I understood its significance.

At the age of eighteen, I left home to attend Bible college. A bell rang throughout the dormitory twice daily—at 6:30 am and at 10:00 pm—to signal an enforced quiet time. Students were to be in their rooms for a half hour of prayer and Bible reading. I complied to follow the rules, not because I appreciated the value of developing prayer as a spiritual discipline.

Years later, as a young mom, I attended a weekly prayer meeting with several other mothers. That's when my understanding about prayer began to deepen. I started to identify several faulty beliefs I had developed over the years about prayer: that it was an activity to be checked off on a daily spiritual to-do list, that it had to be eloquent to be heard, and that it had to fill a certain time length to be most effective—the wordier and the longer, the better.

For years I had struggled with feelings of guilt—that I didn't pray enough. I had also wrestled with feelings of inadequacy—that I didn't pray well enough. I was afraid to pray out loud in public for fear I would do it wrong and not sound spiritual. But everything changed when I began to see prayer as conversing with God.

Prayer isn't our opportunity to impress God or others within earshot. It's not our way of convincing Him to grant our wishes, nor is it a means of earning merit in His eyes. It's the means of growing in relationship with the One who is our very life. It's a two-way conversation with the God of the universe. It's our yes to His invitation to intimacy. It's our acknowledgment we want and need interaction with

Him—not only in emergencies but also in the mundane of everyday life. It's opening our hearts and minds to Him, expressing our love and gratitude to Him, asking Him to cleanse us from anything that grieves Him, welcoming Him to teach us His truth, and inviting Him to guide our path.

Sometimes, this means we tell God everything on our minds. Sometimes, it means we sit in silence because words escape us. It always means we listen for His voice and give Him the opportunity to express Himself. This week, let's take a closer look at the Bible's teaching about prayer. As we do, let's ask the Lord to align our thoughts about prayer with His thoughts.

— DAY 1: THANKSGIVING AND PRAISE

Heavenly Father, thank You for inviting communication with You. Help me to understand prayer for the privilege it is. Amen.

Prayer is God's invitation for you to converse with Him and, ultimately, have greater intimacy with Him. First Place for Health recognizes the importance of prayer to its members' well-being mentally, emotionally, spiritually, and physically. This is why the program encourages you to pray both on an individual basis and for others in your group. Yet while prayer is powerful, it is also often misunderstood. This week's memory verse encourages you to present your requests to God, but it lists one additional action to take. What is that action?

_____

_____

_____

_____

_____

_____

Focusing on your needs can increase your worries about them. Worry is one of the main stress-eating triggers for most people, which reveals the importance of giving thanks—expressing gratitude for what God has already done or will do in accordance with His promises. What does Paul say in Philippians 4:6 is the outcome when you combine thanksgiving with asking?

_____

_____

_____

_____

Visualize this week's verse as a mathematical equation of sorts: *prayer + thanksgiving = peace*. Both elements are of equal necessity. But what happens if you neglect to give thanks?

_____

_____

_____

_____

Read Daniel 6:3–11. Giving thanks might feel difficult at times. What difficulties was Daniel facing? How did he respond (see verse 10)?

_____

_____

_____

_____

For what might Daniel have given thanks, considering his situation?

_____

_____

_____

Read Psalm 100:4. The psalmist says we are to "enter [God's] gates with _____ and his courts with _____; give _____ to him and _____ his name." God commands us to praise Him because He knows that focusing our thoughts on His character will change us for the good. Filling our minds with the truth about who He is will dispel our fears and fill us with courage. It will take the focus off our inadequacies and place it on the One who is more than adequate to meet every need we will ever have. Read Acts 16:22–32. Paul and Silas were innocent, yet the guards locked them in the inner dungeon—a filthy, dark hole reserved for the worst criminals. How did they respond?

_____

_____

_____

_____

Read Psalm 33:1. The King James Version reads, "Rejoice in the Lord, O ye righteous: for praise is comely for the upright." Paul and Silas's ability to praise in dire circumstances was comely, or attractive. What happened as a result? How did their response affect those around them?

_____

_____

_____

How might the outcome have changed if they had chosen to complain or panic?

_____

_____

_____

Prayer is about so much more than just presenting our requests to God. John Heuss describes it this way: "We pray not to get something, but to open up a two-way street between us and God, so that we and others may inwardly become something."[1] Prayer changes us—and thanksgiving and praise help move that process along. This applies to every concern we face, including health issues. Asking God to help you succeed is easy, but for what can you thank and praise God when achieving your wellness goals takes more effort and time than you expected?

_____

_____

_____

Write a prayer below expressing your need for God's help, thanking Him in advance for what He will do, and praising Him for His strength that can overcome food battles.

_____

_____

_____

_____

> *Lord, You are loving, wise, and faithful. Thank You for giving me access to You at any time. I am blessed. Amen.*

— DAY 2: ATTITUDE CHECK

Father, my mind cannot fully comprehend the privilege of prayer. Help me understand it accurately so I might enjoy and develop this gift more. Amen.

Our beliefs about prayer shape our attitudes toward it. For instance, if we believe God answers prayers on the basis of our merit, prayer will become an exercise in strutting our spirituality to impress Him so He will grant our requests. Read Luke 18:9–14 and compare the attitudes of the two men. For what did the Pharisee thank God? What merits did he claim (see verses 11–12)?

_____

_____

_____

_____

_____

_____

What did the tax collector's body language and behavior convey about his attitude? What merit (or lack thereof) did he claim (see verse 13)?

_____

_____

_____

_____

_____

Which of the two attitudes received God's favor (see verse 14)? Why?

_____

_____

_____

_____

Read Daniel 9:17–19. On what basis does this passage say you pray and receive answers?

_____

_____

_____

_____

Another common misunderstanding about prayer is that it means telling God how He should deal with our concerns. I realized my faulty beliefs in this regard when I caught myself praying, "God, You need to do such-and-such in response to this situation." Imagine my telling God how to do His job! The truth is that prayer is not telling God what to do. It's expressing our desires but ultimately surrendering our will to His. It's inviting Him to exercise His wisdom, power, and sovereignty in a way that will bring Him glory. What did Jesus pray in Luke 22:42?

_____

_____

_____

_____

Apply Jesus' example to a situation that causes you concern. "Father, if You are willing, please _____ ; yet not my will, but Yours be done." Now turn to 1 Peter 5:7. What are you to do with your anxieties?

_____

_____

_____

_____

Casting your cares on the Lord means you hurl your concerns onto Him, surrender your desire for control, and trust Him with the outcome. How does knowing God cares for you encourage you to share your desires and fears about your weight loss efforts with Him?

_____

_____

_____

_____

Read Matthew 11:28–30. What promise can you experience when you accept Christ's invitation to deal with your concerns in His wisdom and His way?

_____

_____

_____

_____

James 1:5–6 reveals a third mistaken belief about prayer. What attitudes might you develop toward prayer if you believe God resents you asking Him for help?

_____

_____

_____

_____

_____

What attitudes will you develop toward prayer if you believe He will gladly communicate with you when you come to Him for help?

_____

_____

_____

_____

_____

Heavenly Father, thank You for offering to carry my concerns. Help me to trust You with my whole heart because You care so deeply for me. Amen.

— DAY 3: HINDRANCES TO PRAYER

Lord, grant me an attitude of expectancy—that You will speak to me and I will be able to hear Your voice. Make me aware of and willing to deal with barriers to our communication. Amen.

Sometimes we may feel as though our prayers hit the ceiling and bounce back. We might think it is God's issue—that our prayers are going unheard because He is either cold and distant or too busy to pay attention to us. The truth is that sometimes we can cause our prayers to be hindered. Read the following verses and draw a line from each hindrance to its solution.

HINDRANCE	SOLUTION
Psalm 66:18	Romans 12:10
Mark 6:1–6	Matthew 6:6
Matthew 6:14–15	Mark 11:25
John 13:34	Matthew 26:42
1 Peter 3:7	1 John 1:9
James 4:1-3	James 1:6
Matthew 6:5	Colossians 3:14

Recall a time when you experienced one of the above hindrances to prayer. What action did you take to overcome it?

_____

_____

_____

Read Ezekiel 14:1–3. What hindrance is addressed here?

_____

_____

_____

_____

An *idol* can be defined as anything that takes God's rightful place in your heart. It may be your career, a relationship, a possession, food, or the number on a scale. You can determine whether or not something has become an idol by asking, "How would I respond if God asked me to give this up?" If you cannot allow God full access to it, it's an idol and a hindrance to your prayers.

Take a moment to ask the Holy Spirit to reveal whether you have allowed a person, possession, purpose, or even food to become an idol. If the answer is yes, confess this as sin and invite God to assume His rightful place in your heart. Now turn to Daniel 10:7–14. How does this hindrance to prayer differ from the others?

_____

_____

_____

_____

Who was responsible for this hindrance?

_____

_____

_____

_____

When you are walking in right relationship with God through Jesus Christ, your prayers become a powerful force with an eternal impact. Satan knows this, and he will do everything possible to hinder your prayer life. Busyness is one of the tactics he uses on me. What tactic does he use to hinder your prayer life?

_____

_____

_____

_____

Don't allow Satan to succeed. Commit to doing whatever is necessary to eliminate hindrances to your prayers so you can partner with God in seeing His purposes fulfilled on earth.

> *Heavenly Father, thank You for revealing Your truth. Please give us the desire and strength needed to walk in that truth so we can enjoy unhindered fellowship with You. Amen.*

— DAY 4: WHEN WE DON'T KNOW WHAT TO SAY

Heavenly Father, sometimes words fail me. I'm so thankful that Your power is not limited by the length of my prayers. Amen.

My prayer life changed when I experienced a relationship so hurtful that I felt my heart would literally break. Whenever I'd prayed for other peoples' problems in the past, I had managed eloquent-sounding pleas on their behalf. When I'd faced troubles of my own, I had easily presented to the Lord a lengthy list of possible solutions for fixing them. But this time, the only prayer I could muster was, "Jesus, help!" Eloquent or spiritual-sounding, it was not. Filled with creative problem-solving ideas? No way. Heartfelt and desperate? Yes.

That experience—though something I would never choose to relive—changed my thinking about the prayers to which God listens and responds. I no longer worry about whether or not they're worded correctly. I no longer repeat sentences in varying ways, as though doing so makes them more effective. Now, when faced with challenges that leave me clueless, I utter simple prayers in faith, believing they can move mountains.

Read Psalm 107:4–9. How would you describe the circumstances facing the people mentioned in this passage?

_____

_____

_____

Verse 6 in the *New Living Translation* reads, "'Lord, help!' they cried in their trouble." How do we know God heard their prayer?

_____

_____

_____

Read Psalm 107:10–16. Verse 13 in the *New Living Translation* again reads, "'Lord, help!' they cried in their trouble." What happened when they prayed these words?

_____

_____

_____

_____

Read Psalm 107:17–22. As with the previous two passages, the people cried, "'Lord, help!" (verse 19 NLT). What happened?

_____

_____

_____

_____

Finally, read Psalm 107:23–31. How did God respond to the sailors' plea, "'Lord, help!" (verse 28 NLT)? To which of the above scenarios can you most relate? Why?

_____

_____

_____

_____

When you are facing a crisis, you might find it difficult to string two or three words together, much less an entire sentence. God knows your human frailty, and He has sent help your way. Read Romans 8:26–27. Who helps you in your distress when you don't know what to pray?

_____

_____

_____

_____

Sometimes you might allow your emotions, rather than the truth, dictate what you pray. How do the Holy Spirit's prayers differ from your own?

_____

_____

_____

How does knowing the Holy Spirit is praying for you as you seek to honor God with your body encourage you today?

_____

_____

_____

Read John 17:15–24. Who else is praying for us? What is He praying on your behalf (see verses 15, 17, 21, 24)?

_____

_____

_____

At times you may lack the strength or wisdom to know how to pray, but God's got your back. He knows your heart's cries and cares deeply about you. This is why He has enlisted both Jesus and the Holy Spirit to pray on your behalf. Today, take a few minutes to ponder this amazing truth and to thank God for it.

> *Lord, thank You that both Jesus and the Holy Spirit are interceding on my behalf. Your mercy and kindness astound me. Amen.*

— DAY 5: PRAY ALWAYS

Dear God, I'm humbled and amazed that You invite me into conversation with You. Grant me a responsive heart—one that says "Yes, Lord." Amen.

I recently saw a picture of a pajama-clad boy kneeling at his bedside. With his hands folded and face tilted heavenward, the little fella resembled a cherub basking in God's presence. If only we could all enjoy such precious, uninterrupted time in prayer. Real life, however, calls us to care for others, maintain a household, commute to and from our jobs, be faithful in our workplace, volunteer within our church or community, and make time for our spouse and our own self-care. In the midst of your busy life, what role should prayer play?

_____

_____

_____

_____

Read Colossians 4:2. Paul writes that you are to "_____ yourselves to prayer." Compare with 1 Thessalonians 5:17—you are to "pray _____." Seriously? Devote yourself to prayer? Pray continually? The very thought carries potential for guilt, especially if you believe the key to effective prayer is uninterrupted time on your knees. Mistaken beliefs in this regard will cause you to fall into legalism or defeat, which is not what God intends. In your own words, how would you explain God's intention for prayer?

_____

_____

_____

_____

God's loving intent is for you to maintain ongoing connection with Him. He wants prayer to be as natural to you as breathing. Just as breathing infuses you with life-giving oxygen, so prayer infuses you with spiritual life, peace, wisdom, strength, and joy.

A prayer I breathe frequently is, "Father, My body is Your temple, and Your power at work within me enables me to care for it properly." I often pray this sentence prayer on the run, especially when I'm tempted to grab a quick fix to satisfy an urge for something sweet or savory. It keeps me connected to my Father's heart and reminds me of His ongoing presence.

Read John 15:4–5. How does "praying always" intersect with the teaching about abiding in the Vine? What is one result of maintaining close communication with the Lord?

_____

_____

_____

_____

_____

What actions can you take to enjoy conversation with God that never ends?

_____

_____

_____

_____

_____

_____

In addition to instructing you to pray always, the Bible tells you to pray with perseverance. Read Luke 18:1–5. Satan wants to discourage you from praying, and he will plant seeds of doubt in your mind about God's care for you. Those seeds might grow into thoughts of God being like the judge. What is the judge's attitude toward the widow's persistence (see verses 4–5)?

_____

_____

_____

_____

Now read Ephesians 3:12. How would you contrast the judge's attitude with God's attitude when you come to Him in prayer?

_____

_____

_____

_____

This verse in the *New Living Translation* reads, "Because of Christ and our faith in him, we can come fearlessly into God's presence assured of his glad welcome." On what basis does God welcome you into His presence through prayer?

_____

_____

_____

_____

Circle the words that describe what your response should be. How wonderful to know that God will never tire of our coming to Him in prayer!

Father, thank You for the privilege of ongoing communication with You. I am forever grateful. Amen.

— DAY 6: REFLECTION AND APPLICATION

Heavenly Father, thank You for Your holy Word and the power it contains. Teach me how to harness that power through prayer. Amen.

Previously, I mentioned that my prayer life grew when I began attending a weekly prayer meeting. That is where I learned to pray using God's Word, and it transformed my conversations with Him. Quite honestly, they had become stale, and I was hungry for change. My usual go-to sounded something like this: "God, bless my kids and keep them safe today." Beyond that, I felt stymied. Using God's Word presented me with endless topics and ideas.

Proverbs 3:1–4 became a favorite for me. Based on these verses, I prayed, "Heavenly Father, teach my children to store Your commands in their heart. Teach them to wear love and faithfulness around their necks and to write them on the tablet of their hearts. As they do this, keep Your promise to grant them favor in Your sight and in the sight of man. Thank You in advance for what You will do in and through their lives. Amen."

Proverbs 2:2–5 became another favorite. "Lord," I prayed, "You value wisdom, so tune my children's hearts to value wisdom and understanding. Create in them an insatiable desire to search for it as diligently as they would hunt for hidden treasure. Fulfill Your promise that they will discover what it means to fear You and gain an intimate knowledge of who You are." I added, "Please do this, Lord. If my kids give You the honor and respect You deserve, and if they possess an intimate knowledge of who You are, then every issue they will ever face will be resolved in a way that will glorify You. Every major decision they make will bring You joy."

When I incorporated God's Word into my prayers—being careful to not take it out of context—I knew beyond a doubt that I was praying according to the Father's will. I presented my requests to Him with confidence, believing He would answer. Of course, I realized the Lord's answer might not look like how I thought it should and that it might not happen in the time frame I preferred. But I knew the answer would come according to His schedule and wisdom.

Praying God's Word will present you with infinite themes and subjects to address. Read Psalm 44:4–8, 138:8, and 139:13–18. Write a prayer below about your wellness journey using one of these passages as its basis.

_____

_____

_____

_____

_____

In Ephesians 3:14–21, Paul records his prayer for Christ's followers living in Ephesus. Read this passage and linger on each phrase so you can absorb its beauty and life-transforming potential. Now write it as a prayer below either for yourself or someone you know.

_____

_____

_____

_____

_____

God, I praise You for Your indescribable love. Who am I that You are mindful of me? And yet You love me and invite ongoing conversation with me. I'm humbled, honored, and grateful. Amen.

— DAY 7: REFLECTION AND APPLICATION

Holy God, it's easy for me to make prayer a one-sided conversation. Help me to remember otherwise and give me a quiet heart to hear Your voice. Amen.

Charles Stanley states, "To have God speak to the heart is a majestic experience, an experience that people may miss if they monopolize the conversation and never pause to hear God's responses."[2] I recall one morning when I felt particularly exhausted. My husband was the program director at a Christian camp on British Columbia's coast at the time. I supported him in his role, maintained our household and our three kids' busy schedules, volunteered in church programs, and wrote for several magazines. Was it any wonder fatigue struck?

My body, brain, and spirit needed rest. That morning, I felt compelled to sit in solitude and silence on a rocky point that jutted into a saltwater harbor near our home. I had no agenda other than to listen for God's voice. What might He want to say to me? At first my thoughts raced to menu ideas for dinner. I lassoed them, but they wrestled free and dashed off to recall a conversation I'd had the day before. I reeled them in, but they escaped again. The struggle continued for several minutes.

Suddenly, I heard a whoosh overhead. I looked up and saw several herons—they had taken flight from their perches in the towering evergreens behind me. Minutes later, a mink climbed ashore inches from my feet. He stared at me for a few seconds before ducking beneath a log. Then a trio of porpoise swam past.

The nature show left me feeling as though the Creator had lavished His love on me. I wanted to sit there for hours, but real life called. "How should I spend the rest of my day?" I asked Him. A thought came to mind: *Write an article about dating your kids.*

My husband and I had dated our kids for Saturday breakfasts when they were younger, and they loved it. I returned to the house and spent three hours writing the article in hopes that other parents would read it and incorporate the tradition. My phone rang the instant I finished. The caller was the editor of a well-known family magazine for which I wrote often. "Do you have anything for me?" she asked.

God spoke to my heart that day, and that experience helped align my thoughts about prayer with His. Prayer is more than telling Him about our needs, wants, and worries, especially if we're in crisis mode. It's a dialogue, not a monologue. It's a two-way conversation in which we talk with God, not at God. And that means we practice the art of being quiet and listening.

Today, spend a few minutes in quiet with God. Invite Him to speak to you about your wellness journey. What does He want your eating habits to look like? How does He want you to exercise your body? What does He want your weight goal to be?

Lord, teach me to be still in Your presence, if only for a few minutes. Train my ears to hear Your voice and speak to Me. Amen.

WEEK FOUR: REFRAMING OBEDIENCE

SCRIPTURE MEMORY VERSE

Observe what the Lord your God requires: Walk in obedience to him, and keep his decrees and commands, his laws and regulations, as written in the Law of Moses. Do this so that you may prosper in all you do and wherever you go.

1 Kings 2:3

The word *obedience* earned a bad rap with me when I was a teen. My parents asked me to do things I didn't want to do, and I felt like their rules encroached on my rights. Having to respect a midnight curfew on Saturdays topped the list.

My mind equated obedience with "killjoy." I believed my folks were old-fashioned. Clearly, they didn't understand my needs and wanted to spoil my fun. I envied my friends whose parents let them stay out as long as they wanted. Why couldn't mine be like theirs?

Inaccurate thinking led to wrong behavior. I chose to ignore the curfew they had set in lieu of my own—not just once, but multiple times. My disobedience didn't work so well!

My thinking changed when I became a parent. I loved my kids and wanted to protect them from doing something that might cause them pain. So I set rules. It grieved me if they chose to disregard those parameters. Why would they trust their limited understanding rather than the wisdom their father and I gained through time and experience?

In the spiritual context, God is our Father and cares deeply about our overall well-being. He sets rules for us and urges us to obey them. He doesn't do this because He is a joy-stealer but because He knows we will benefit from following them. But there's more to this topic of obedience than just following rules.

Obeying God also involves saying yes when He asks us to do something that doesn't make sense or seems beyond our abilities. He wants to develop our full potential, and giving us faith-stretching tasks helps accomplish His desire. Saying yes to Him allows us the privilege of experiencing His power, provision, and guidance in new ways. It always guarantees we will have a deeper understanding of His character. It will also lead us into greater intimacy with Him—the very thing for which He created us.

In this week's study, we will mine Scripture to discover gems of truth about obedience. We will see what God says about it—why He values it, what happens when we do what He asks, and what happens when we don't obey Him.

— DAY 1: PUTTING OBEDIENCE INTO PROPER PERSPECTIVE

Lord, please align my thoughts about obedience with Yours. Help me see it as a benefit, not as a restraint, and to respond in a way that honors You. Amen.

The creation story relates how the world came into being. It also demonstrates God's authority over every created thing. Read the following verses in Genesis 1. Write God's command in the first column, and then record creation's response in the second column.

VERSE	GOD'S COMMAND	CREATION'S RESPONSE
3		
6		
9		
11		
14		

This pattern continues as all of creation surrenders to God's authority. What does God say the outcome is in verse 31?

_____

Psalm 104 paints another word picture of God's authority over creation. He sets the earth's foundation and the sea's boundaries (see verses 5–9). He commands water to flow and plants to produce food (see verses 10–15). He rules the moon and sun to ensure day and night and seasons (see verses 19–23). How does creation benefit from God's rule (see verses 13, 28, 30)?

_____

In verse 24, we read, "In wisdom [God] made them all." A.W. Tozer defines wisdom as "the ability to devise perfect ends and to achieve those ends by the most perfect means. It sees the end from the beginning, so there can be no need to guess or conjecture."[1] Read Psalm 147:5, 40:28, and Romans 11:33–36. How do these verses describe God's wisdom?

_____

God created all things in His infinite wisdom. He designed us, so He knows what is best for us, and His intent toward us is always good. His wisdom—combined with His love, faithfulness, and holiness—makes Him completely trustworthy. We have seen how creation's surrender to God produced a good outcome. But everything changed when Adam and Eve chose to disobey. Read Genesis 2:15–17 and 3:1–6. What command did God issue? How did Adam and Eve respond?

___

Read Genesis 2:7–10, 14–24. What was the outcome? What did Adam and Eve's behavior reveal about their thoughts about God?

___

Adam and Eve doubted God's character, and those doubts caused them to question His intent toward Him. Wrong thinking led to sin, and the outcome was not good. What parallels can you draw between this account and your life?

___

God created you to flourish, and surrendering your will to Him—because He is all-wise—is the key to making this happen. Read Deuteronomy 4:39–40. What is the promise God makes to those who obey Him? What is the condition?

_____

_____

_____

What is one area in which God is asking you to obey Him? What is hindering your obedience? How will obedience benefit you spiritually, mentally, emotionally, and physically? How does knowing God is infinitely wise change your thinking?

_____

_____

_____

> *Father God, You are Creator, and I am Your creation. Please grant me a correct understanding of the depth of Your wisdom and a heart to walk in surrender to Your commands. Amen.*

— DAY 2: ATTITUDE IS EVERYTHING

Lord God, help me view obedience as You do—as something to do joyfully rather than with a negative sense of obligation. Amen.

My son and his wife have seven children with another on the way. I admire the job they're doing as parents, especially in teaching their kids to obey promptly and with a positive attitude. There is a big difference between agreeing to do something and actually doing it. There is also a big difference between obeying cheerfully and obeying reluctantly. Attitude is everything when it comes to children obeying their parents. The same is true as we relate to God and His commands.

WEEK FOUR REFRAMING OBEDIENCE

A common misperception is that half-hearted obedience is somehow better than blatant disobedience. Another misperception is that it is okay to pick and choose which of God's commands we want to obey. King Saul fell into this category. Read his story in 1 Samuel 15:1–21. What did God tell Saul to do (see verse 3)? How did Saul respond (see verses 8–9)?

_____

_____

_____

How did Saul justify his behavior (see verses 13, 15, 20)? What did Samuel say in response to Saul's misperceptions about obedience (see verses 22–23)?

_____

_____

_____

What was the outcome of Saul's disobedience (see verse 35)?

_____

_____

Saul's mistaken beliefs resulted in a heartbreaking outcome. His story could have had a much different ending if only he had fully and joyfully obeyed God. In Psalm 40:8, the psalmist writes, "I take joy in doing your will" (NLT). Compare with Joshua 1:8. What helped the psalmist develop this attitude?

_____

_____

_____

In the midst of your busy life, what intentional actions can you take to write God's law on your heart so that you, too, might develop joy in doing His will?

_____

_____

_____

The author of Psalm 119 reveals his deep respect and love for God's commands. His words in this psalm contain numerous nuggets of truth. What do the following verses tell you about the attitude with which you should regard God's commands?

VERSE	
4-7	
20	
30	
32	
47-48	
60	
109-112	
167	

WEEK FOUR **REFRAMING OBEDIENCE**

Obeying God with a joyful heart results in even greater joy because God will reward you for doing what He says with the right attitude. Look again at Psalm 119 and list those rewards.

VERSE	
1-2	
9	
35	
45	
165	

In verse 55, the psalmist writes, "I reflect at night on who you are, O LORD, and I obey your law because of this" (NLT). Based on this insight, what should your motive be for obeying God?

_____

_____

_____

_____

Read verse 73. Why does God's role as your Creator deserve your willing and joyful obedience? Apply this to your wellness journey. What commands would be wise to follow to promote good health? With what attitude should you embrace those commands?

_____

_____

_____

_____

Father, grant me a heart that eagerly embraces Your commands. Help me value obedience as You do. Amen.

— DAY 3: THE PORTAL TO PEACE

Heavenly Father, thank You for caring about my well-being and for the gift of peace that comes through surrendering to You. Amen.

We might mistakenly believe we will experience peace if we are free to do whatever we want. In reality, peace comes when we align our will with God's will for our lives. Read Isaiah 48:17–22. What two things does God say He yearns to do for you (see verse 17)? What two blessings does God long to give you if only you would obey (see verse 18)?

_____

_____

_____

_____

WEEK FOUR **REFRAMING OBEDIENCE**

Psalm 119 mentions numerous benefits for obeying God's commands. Read the following verses and list those benefits.

VERSE	
1-2	
3	
6	
9	
45	
80	
93	
98-100	
104	

Read verse 165. Which of the blessings is mentioned again in Isaiah 48:18?

_____

_____

_____

What is your definition of *peace*?

_____

_____

The Hebrew word for *peace* is *shalom*. This word denotes the wholeness, tranquility, perfection, and prosperity of every good thing. Wouldn't you love to experience this deep, settled state of mind and heart on an ongoing basis? The good news is you can! But as these verses state, there is a condition: you must _____ God's law.

One writer put it this way: "To love a law may seem strange, but it is the only true divine life. To keep it because we are afraid of its penalties is only a form of fear. . . . To keep it to preserve a good name may be propriety and respectability. . . . To keep it because we love it is to show that it is already part of us—it has entered into the moral texture of our being. Sin then becomes distasteful, and temptations lose their power."[2]

What would your life look like if specific temptations no longer held power over you? Finish the following sentences. (An example is given below.)

If temptation and sin lost their power over me, I would . . .
never again wrestle with bingeing in secret.

If temptation and sin lost their power over me, I would . . .

If temptation and sin lost their power over me, I would . . .

If temptation and sin lost their power over me, I would . . .

These declarations can become a reality if you love God's law and make it part of the moral texture of your being. This happens when you ask God to give you an appreciation for its life-saving and life-changing truth—and through obedience. There are no shortcuts. Once you experience shalom peace as a result of obedience, sin becomes distasteful and temptations lose their power.

Father God, grant me the willingness to obey You in all things. My restless heart craves the shalom peace You've promised. Amen.

— DAY 4: FROM LOVE COMES OBEDIENCE

Dear God, paint for me a true picture of who You are and Your love for me, and then help me to respond as You deserve. Amen.

God never created us to be robots programmed to do His bidding. His design for humankind is quite the opposite! He wants an intimate relationship with us. As Bible teacher Nancy DeMoss Wolgemuth states, "The sovereign Creator God ruled over His creation with tender love, inviting His creatures to engage with Him in a divine dance-of-sorts, in which He led and they followed. They responded to His initiative with trust, love, and surrender."[3]

Everything changed when the created misconstrued the Creator's love and intent toward them. The battle for control has raged ever since, but God relentlessly pursues and woos us so we might return to a relationship in which we love and obey Him in response to His loving us. Read John 3:16. To what degree did God demonstrate His love for us?

_____

_____

_____

_____

God held nothing back in loving us, and we are to love Him in the same way. Read Mark 12:30. What is a practical example of loving God with all your heart? Soul? Mind? Strength?

_____

_____

_____

For me, this idea of loving God with all my strength assumed new meaning when I resolved to get serious about my health. It now means saying no to sleeping in and, instead, rising at 5:30 AM to work out for an hour before breakfast. I offer the time spent exercising as my love offering to Him. What can you give as a love offering to God? Write John 14:15 here. Circle the word that proves your love for Christ.

_____

_____

_____

Sometimes fear overshadows our love for the Lord. We might be afraid that doing what He says will require personal sacrifice. *What if He asks us to give away a portion of our hard-earned money or possessions? What if He asks us to serve Him in a dangerous or faraway place?* Does the thought of obeying God make you afraid? Explain.

_____

_____

_____

At times, our pride outweighs our love for the Lord. We want to honor God, but not enough to humble ourselves or risk our reputation. Has pride hindered you from obedience? Explain.

_____

_____

_____

An inaccurate understanding of God's love can also hinder you from obeying Him. Read Romans 8:31–39 aloud. Make it personal by replacing the pronouns *we, our,* and *us* with *I, me, mine,* and *my.* Now read Paul's prayer in Ephesians 3:14–19. How does God's love change you (see verse 19)?

_____

_____

_____

_____

_____

God's sacrificial love deserves your best response—to love Him with every part of who you are and to demonstrate that love through your obedience to His commands.

> *Father, thank You for loving me deeply. The least I can do is love You in return. Amen.*

— DAY 5: OBEDIENCE COMES WITH A PRICE TAG

Lord, thank You for modeling obedience despite the cost. Your example inspires me to do no less. Amen.

It is easy to think that Jesus, being fully God, had the authority and freedom to do whatever He wished when He became a man and lived on earth. The Bible, however, says He lived a life marked by obedience. Based on John 8:28–29 and 15:10, who did He obey? In what ways?

_____

_____

_____

_____

Andrew Murray defined humility as "the sense of entire nothingness, which comes when we see how truly God is all, and in which we make way for God to be all."[4] Just imagine! Jesus—the Creator and Sustainer of life—only spoke and did what His Father told Him to say and do. His attitude and actions made a way for His Father to be all. Read Philippians 2:6–8. What did Christ's obedience cost Him?

_____

_____

_____

What attitude enabled Jesus to obey His Father in all things (see verses 7–8)?

_____

_____

_____

Christ's obedience led to His being mocked, beaten, and killed. Shortly before His arrest, He agonized over His impending crucifixion. Read Luke 22:42 and write out His prayer. Underline the words that show His resolve to honor God's will at all cost.

_____

_____

_____

_____

Read Hebrews 5:7–9. What did Jesus learn from suffering?

_____

_____

_____

Jesus' suffering taught Him obedience. This doesn't mean He had been disobedient in the past. He had perfect theoretical knowledge about the importance of obedience, but He experienced it when He became human. Jesus understands how difficult it is for us to obey, but He proved we can obey even when it is hard. Read Philippians 2:13. What is the key to your ability to obey Him in every area of your life? How does this truth relate specifically to your First Place for Health journey?

_____

_____

_____

_____

Read Romans 5:17. What did Christ's obedience accomplish?

_____

_____

Read Philippians 2:9-11. How did God honor Christ for His obedience?

_____

_____

_____

What might obeying Christ cost you in terms of being a wise steward of your body?

_____

_____

_____

Replacing old, familiar habits with a new, healthy lifestyle requires obedience, and it comes with a cost. Saying no to favorite comfort foods and refusing second helpings might hurt emotionally. Exercise might hurt physically—at least for a while. Read 1 Peter 3:14. What promise is made to those who do what is right despite suffering for it?

_____

_____

_____

How might your obedience in the physical realm benefit other people? How might God honor your obedience to make your body a living sacrifice to Him?

> *Father, thank You for making me an overcomer when I surrender to You. Amen.*

— DAY 6: REFLECTION AND APPLICATION

Father, forgive me for the times I have thought myself wiser than You. Cleanse me from the sin of disobedience and help me live according to Your will. Amen.

On Day 2, we looked at the story of Saul and his thoughts about obedience. God gave him clear marching orders for battle, but he tweaked them to his liking instead of obeying them completely. When Samuel then confronted him, Saul tried to justify his actions.

It's easy to judge Saul, but aren't we prone to do the same thing? Maybe God tells us to forgive someone who has hurt us (see Ephesians 4:32), but we tweak the order to our liking: "Sure, I'll forgive, but on one condition—she asks for it first." Then we justify our response: "She's the one who hurt me, so she needs to make the first move."

Or maybe God tells us to give thanks at all times (see 1 Thessalonians 5:18), but we decide to change the order to suit us. We express gratitude when the going is easy but let our emotions rule when life becomes an uphill climb. We grumble and complain, and then justify our attitude: I don't deserve this hardship, God. I did nothing wrong.

Or God tells us to avoid the sin of gluttony (see Proverbs 23:20–21), but we adjust the command to suit us and eat as whim dictates. We may justify our behavior by saying, "I couldn't help myself—everything tasted so yummy. Besides, the cook slaved to prepare the meal, and I didn't want to disappoint her by not enjoying it."

Saul paid the consequences for failing to obey God wholeheartedly. The same is true for us. Refusing to forgive results in resentment. Refusing to give thanks at all times turns us into whiny people with a negative outlook. And refusing to control our appetite turns us into unhealthy people who are unhappy with the way we look and feel.

Disobedience builds a barrier between us and the Lord. The relationship suffers, our joy fades, and our peace disappears. But the moment we acknowledge our wrongdoing and align our hearts with God's, He restores us to a right relationship that causes us to flourish.

MYplace O BIBLE STUDY

Psalm 32 portrays this truth. Take a few moments to read King David's account. How did disobedience affect him? (Compare with his experience once he chose to change his ways.)

_____

_____

_____

Linger on verse 8: "I will instruct you and teach you in the way you should go; I will counsel you with my loving eye on you." How do these words assure you that God deserves your trust and enthusiastic obedience?

_____

_____

_____

As honestly as you can, write a prayer confessing any area in your life where you have walked contrary to God's commands. Ask Him for the desire to obey and the power to help you do it.

_____

_____

_____

_____

Father, You are completely trustworthy. Help me to obey Your instructions and counsel. Amen.

— DAY 7: REFLECTION AND APPLICATION

Lord, You are God and I am not. Teach me to obey even when I don't understand the reason behind Your commands. Amen.

Occasionally, God will tell us to do things that don't make sense. Just put yourself in Noah's sandals and imagine how he felt when God said, "Build an ark, and fill it with two of every species of bird and animal" (see Genesis 6:13–21). A lesser man might have said, "A what? You're kidding, right? You'd better find someone else for the job, because this sounds a bit crazy." Read Genesis 6:22. How did Noah respond? (Compare with Genesis 7:5.)

_____

_____

_____

Read Genesis 6:9–10. What in Noah's character enabled him to say yes to this mammoth task? What was the outcome of his obedience (see Genesis 7:23; 9:1, 8)?

_____

_____

_____

God also gave Joshua unusual instructions. Read Joshua 6:1–5. What were those instructions?

_____

_____

_____

How might Joshua have felt about doing battle using rams' horns rather than traditional weapons of warfare? How did he respond (see verse 6)?

_____

_____

_____

What was the outcome of Joshua's willingness to do what God said (see verses 20–21, 27)?

_____

_____

_____

Then there's Abraham. Read Genesis 22:2. What did God command him to do? How might he have felt?

_____

_____

_____

How did he respond (see verses 3–10)? What did his response indicate about his love for God (see verse 12)?

_____

_____

_____

WEEK FOUR REFRAMING OBEDIENCE

What was the outcome of his obedience (see verses 16–18)?

___

I'm grateful for Bible characters such as these who teach us about trusting and obeying God even when we don't understand. As I write this study, my husband and I are preparing to move onto a forty-eight foot sailboat. We've watched God weave our life experiences together with our interests to bring us to this point. We've said yes, but it has come with a cost.

We're in the process of sorting our possessions and getting rid of almost everything we own. We'll keep a few treasures, such as family photos, for as long as God keeps us on the boat, but the furniture will have to go. We will no longer have sufficient space for our kids and grandkids to gather for an overnighter. We won't have a washer and dryer on board, which means scheduling trips to the laundromat. We will likely have to take showers in the marina's facilities rather than on the boat when we're at shore. So much for ease and privacy.

We have no idea why God is directing us to make such a significant transition, but we're choosing to trust and obey. We've walked with Him long enough to understand His words in Isaiah 55:8–9. What do these verses say about God's thoughts compared to your thoughts? How do they apply to your current situation?

___

God's got your back when He asks you to do something that doesn't make sense to you. May He grant you the desire to obey and then empower you to walk it out.

Father, Your thoughts are higher than our thoughts. Give us Your mind, and then use us for Your highest glory. Amen.

WEEK FIVE: WHAT DOES GOD THINK ABOUT ME?

SCRIPTURE MEMORY VERSE

How precious to me are your thoughts, God! How vast is the sum of them! Were I to count them, they would outnumber the grains of sand—when I awake, I am still with you.

                                                                Psalm 139:17–18

The majority of my published writing is devotional in nature—short pieces that call for a strict word count. So when I sensed the Holy Spirit nudging me to write a chapter book about overcoming fear, I declined.[1] "Who, me?" I said. "I could never find enough words to fill ten chapters and string them together logically." Thoughts of inadequacy messed with my mind for a year and hindered me from saying yes to God's assignment.

If only I had known then what I know now. I now understand I had developed wrong thinking about myself in my childhood. I compared myself with more popular peers and those who consistently won academic achievement awards. This comparison trap turned me into my own worst critic. Nothing I did was good enough—I wasn't pretty enough, or talented enough, or smart enough. Experiencing a broken engagement in my college years only reinforced the lies: I wasn't good enough to keep a man, and obviously something was wrong with me.

These faulty thoughts traveled with me into marriage: I couldn't keep my fiancé, so what made me believe I could keep a husband? Jealousy and fear plagued me when my husband spoke with other women. This wrong thinking also carried into my role as a mother: I worried about ruining the kids and not raising them properly. I tried to better my mothering skills by volunteering for every extra-curricular known to man.

At the same time, I played piano on my church's worship team, taught piano lessons, developed a home daycare business, and served as Sunday school superintendent. Crazy. Subconsciously, I believed my worth was based on performance. I became a human sponge, soaking up others' positive affirmation: "Wow, Grace, how do you do it all? You're amazing!"

Truth be told, I wasn't amazing; I was a hamster chained to a treadmill, going nowhere fast. Freedom came when I began to understand my identity in light of God's thoughts about me.

I'm grateful for the Holy Spirit's persistence in nudging me to write the book. That year-long struggle forced me to align my thoughts with the truth. Understanding God's view of me gave me the courage to say yes to His assignment. I experienced His empowerment and discovered sweet intimacy with Him as a result.

This week's study will help you identify common misperceptions about who you are and replace lies with God's truth. Friends, I implore you to cooperate with God's Spirit as He teaches you through the Word. Allow it to renew your mind and transform you into the person He designed you to be. Are you ready to change your mind for good? Let's get started.

— DAY 1: YOU ARE MY MASTERPIECE

Father, help me train my mind to think about myself in a way that honors You as my Creator. Amen.

How many times have you felt dissatisfied with your appearance or interpersonal skills? How many times have you wished you were someone else—someone more poised, talented, attractive, or influential?

I've lost count of how many times I've felt that way about myself. Maybe you, like me, have looked in the mirror and groaned, "Ugh. I need a makeover!" I've also berated myself for something I said, or neglected to say, in conversations past. I've even caught myself thinking, *You're such an idiot*, when recalling a clumsy move or social faux pas.

How easy it is to criticize and demean ourselves. But consider that doing so insults our Creator. In Ephesians 2:10, Paul says, "For we are God's _____, created in Christ Jesus to do good works, which God prepared in advance for us to do" (NIV).

The New Living Translation translates handiwork as masterpiece. The Greek word for masterpiece is *poema*—the same word from which we get the word poem.

It denotes one who has an artistic flair or extraordinary ability to create a literary masterpiece.

You, my friend, are God's poem, His literary masterpiece. When you placed your faith in Christ for salvation, He invested His finest creative abilities in you. You're His priceless work of art, and He put His signature on you when He gave you His Holy Spirit. Do you believe it?

Identify the thoughts you think about yourself. How do they compare to the truth about your being God's priceless handiwork?

_____

_____

_____

_____

For years, I lived from the lie that my worth came from performance. I thought the busier I was, the more significant I would be. Or that the closer my performance came to perfection, the more acceptable others would find me. My understanding was totally skewed, and I lived under the self-imposed pressure of trying to measure up to imaginary and unattainable standards. Understanding and applying the truth changed everything. *Read Genesis 1:27 and Psalm 139:1–6, 13–16. What gives you significance and worth?*

_____

_____

_____

_____

What's the common denominator in the following verses?

VERSE	COMMON DENOMINATOR
John 3:16	
Romans 5:5	
Romans 5:6-8	
Romans 7:5-6	
1 Corinthians 3:16	
Ephesians 1:4-7	

Based on the above verses, what three things bring you significance?

_____

_____

_____

Performance and busy schedules won't give you significance. It comes from the fact that God loves you, Jesus died for you, and the Holy Spirit lives in you. These are the truths from which God wants you to live. Satan does battle with your mind to thwart God's purposes for you. The moment you recognize his lies, say aloud, "God loves me, Jesus died for me, and the Holy Spirit lives in me. By His power, I will live from these truths."

Dear God, help me live from the truth that I am Your creative and precious handiwork. Amen.

— DAY 2: YOU ARE LOVED

Heavenly Father, the depth of Your love for me boggles my mind. Help me understand it more accurately so its power can transform me. Amen.

It was always a treat to visit my maternal grandparents on their southern Saskatchewan farm. Grandpa wore denim overalls and barn smells. He would plop onto a kitchen chair after doing chores and say to me, "Come here, Gracie." When I came close, he would pull me onto his lap, wrap his arms around me, and give me hugs and whisker rubs. I wiggled and wrestled and faked an attempt to escape. But that was only for show, and he knew it. I adored him, and he adored me. When he died the day before my eleventh birthday, I thought my world had fallen apart.

Grandpa's love for me ran deep, but it paled in comparison to God's love for His children. How would you describe God's love? List as many one-word descriptions as you can.

_____

_____

_____

_____

WEEK FIVE　WHAT DOES GOD THINK ABOUT ME?

Now let's see how the Bible describes God's love and how He demonstrates it. Read the following verses and complete the chart.

VERSE	DESCRIPTION	DEMONSTRATION
Deuteronomy 7:9		
Jeremiah 31:3		
Psalm 86:15		
Zephaniah 3:17		
Romans 5:5		
Romans 8:37–39		
1 John 3:1		

How have you seen God demonstrate His love to you in the past week?

_____

_____

_____

God's love is an indisputable fact of Scripture, and it reflects His nature. It's always faithful because He is faithful. It's always pure because He is pure. It's wise and fair because He is wise and fair. That said, we need to note a truth we sometimes forget or overlook—God lavishes constant love on those who love and obey Him, but not so much for those who reject Him. This doesn't contradict the truth that He is love. Rather, it underscores the truth that He is holy and must punish sin. Compare Deuteronomy 7:9–10 with Deuteronomy 5:9–10. What must you do to receive the fullness of His love?

_____

_____

_____

We are enemies of God until we choose to believe that His Son, Jesus, paid the penalty for our sin. Read Romans 5:6–11. What mind-blowing action did God take to make friendship with Him possible? What was your state apart from Christ (see verses 6, 8, 10)?

_____

_____

_____

To what extent did God go to show His love for you?

_____

_____

_____

What does this tell you about His thoughts toward you?

_____

_____

_____

The Bible is jam-packed with stories that show God's love for sinners. Check out these examples of notorious people with whom Jesus associated: Luke 17:11–19, 19:10–10, and John 4:5–30. How did Jesus demonstrate the Father's love? How did the people respond?

_____

_____

_____

Have you responded to Christ? If not, acknowledge that He paid your sin penalty to make friendship with God possible. Invite Him into your life and to take control. He is crazy in love with you, my friend!

Father God, thank You for loving me even while I was a sinner. I receive Your love and choose to love You in return. Amen.

—— DAY 3: YOU ARE BEING TRANSFORMED

Dear Lord, thank You for seeing beyond my mistakes and messes. Thank You for seeing me for who I will become as You make me more like Jesus. Amen.

I see my grandchildren every two or three months. I'm amazed at how much they change between visits. Their development involves physical growth, of course, but it also involves emotional, mental, and spiritual maturity. Their personalities are becoming more pronounced and their unique giftedness is emerging. They are able to express themselves and engage in more meaningful conversations as time passes.

A child's transformation is a beautiful process to behold. So is ours.

Our thoughts might tell us that change is impossible, especially when we're dealing with a painful past, persistent health issues, or negative attitudes and behaviors that are holding us in bondage. But God is bigger and faithful and gives us a hope-filled future. He designed us for growth, and He delights in seeing it happen in every facet of our lives. Read 2 Corinthians 5:17. Where does lasting transformation begin? What does it mean to be "in Christ"?

_____

_____

_____

Read 1 John 1:9 and Romans 8:1–2. What does God do to set you on the path to becoming a new person?

_____

_____

_____

Society suggests taking self-improvement courses to bring transformation. These can be helpful, but ultimately lasting change comes by having a relationship with God through Jesus Christ. He forgives our sin and gives us a clean slate. He removes our condemnation and sets us free from sin's power. But that's not all! Read Galatians 2:20 and compare with Romans 8:11. What else happens to promote this transformation?

_____

_____

_____

Imagine! Jesus takes up residence in us when we place our faith in Him. The Spirit that raised Christ from the dead works in us! Read Ephesians 1:18–20. How would you describe the power that is at work within those who have a relationship with Jesus?

_____

_____

_____

Read Philippians 4:13. What does Christ's power in you enable you to do?

_____

_____

_____

Jesus' power works in you to make you more like Him, but you also have a role in this process. Read Romans 8:5-6. How would you describe that role?

_____

_____

_____

What outcome can you expect if you let your sinful nature control your mind? Contrast with the promised outcome if the Holy Spirit controls your thoughts. What practical actions can you take to give the Spirit control over your mind?

_____

_____

_____

Identify several attitudes or behaviors in your life that need to align with God's truth. Write them here. Using a different color pen, write the words "I am being transformed by Christ's power in me" across them.

_____

_____

_____

Transformation also requires you to take responsibility for making godly choices. Read Romans 8:12–16. What happens if you continue in your old sinful ways? What is the outcome if you turn from them (see verse 13)?

_____

_____

_____

What are some of the "old" ways you have abandoned? What "new" ways have replaced the old on your wellness journey?

_____

_____

_____

Father, change me from the inside out. Make me more like You. Amen.

— DAY 4: YOU ARE MY AMBASSADOR

Lord, it's a privilege to represent You. Teach me how to be the best ambassador I can be for Your sake. Amen.

Imagine what our lives could look like if we truly understood our identity and significance. We would become world changers. We would fling off every weight and worry, dance in fearless freedom, and never again be defined by a number on a scale.

Satan knows the danger we pose to him when we live from the truth, so he does battle with our minds to distract us and destroy us with lies. Here's a sampling of the lies he planted in my head: *You're a nobody. You have nothing to offer. You serve no purpose. You don't matter.* Sound familiar?

Nothing could be further from the truth. But what exactly is that truth? What does God think about us in relation to His eternal plan for mankind? Read 2 Corinthians 5:18–20. Your God-given role is as His ambassador. How would you define this word?

_____

_____

_____

To summarize, an ambassador is his or her government's highest-ranking representative while living in a foreign country. This person is appointed by his or her country's leader and given authority to speak on that leader's behalf. An ambassador develops healthy relationships with the locals and serves as a liaison between his or her homeland and the country to which he or she has moved. Read Philippians 3:20 and 1 Peter 2:9, 11–12. How does this description apply to you?

_____

_____

_____

According to 2 Corinthians 5:18–21, what message has God given you to speak on His behalf?

_____

_____

_____

Name one person with whom you can share this message. Write a prayer below asking God to prepare that person's heart, provide an opportunity for you to speak truth with love, and give you the words to say.

_____

_____

_____

God has appointed you to bring a message of hope and salvation to the world. He has entrusted you with a task that literally rescues people from death. What does that say about His opinion of you? How would you compare this to your view of yourself?

_____

_____

_____

Here is another misperception within the context of today's discussion: *I'm just an ordinary person. What do I know about being God's ambassador? Sharing the message of hope and salvation is best left to the experts—pastors, church leaders, and missionaries.* Consider that when you reach your goal weight, people take notice. They want to know your secret for success. This presents the perfect opportunity for you to share Christ's message of hope.

Read 1 Corinthians 1:27. Paul wrote these words when the Roman Empire considered Christians a weak bunch of religious idiots. But the believers in Corinth took them by surprise. These common, everyday men and women lived by God's power and changed history. Compare 1 Corinthians 1:27 with 2 Corinthians 12:8–11. It's easy to think of your weaknesses—whether real or perceived—as a detriment in your service to God. What are some personal characteristics or conditions you consider weaknesses? How does God view them?

_____

_____

_____

God looks beyond your weaknesses. He sees them as opportunities for you to experience His wisdom, power, and grace in new ways and for Him to receive the glory. Today, ask Him to give you that same perspective.

> *Father God, thank You for entrusting me with the task of representing You. I am honored. Amen.*

— DAY 5: YOU ARE EMPOWERED

Dear God, thank You for giving me strength to persevere in hardships and accomplish everything You assign, no matter how impossible it seems. Amen.

Have you ever felt weak and inadequate? Maybe parenting a strong-willed or prodigal child has worn you down. Perhaps holding your marriage together has left you depleted. Maybe your job, or caring for an aging parent, or trying to shed unwanted pounds, has wearied you.

We all experience situations or seasons that leave us feeling weak. Our natural tendency is to focus on our circumstances. Unless the Holy Spirit controls our mind, we soon start thinking, *This is too hard. I can't do this anymore.*

My husband and I were living in a three-story townhouse when I lost my mobility. Every evening, I hoisted myself backward up fifteen stairs to reach my bedroom. One night, my thoughts spiraled downward. This is too hard, I said to myself. I can't do this anymore. In that moment, I heard the Holy Spirit whisper, "That's a lie. Speak the truth."

These words came to mind: "I can do all this through [Christ] who gives me strength" (Philippians 4:13). In my situation, "all this" included hoisting myself up those stairs at bedtime. Focusing on truth rather than on my challenges empowered me to persevere until my mobility returned. What does "all this" currently mean for you?

_____

_____

_____

Judges 6 tells of a man who allowed his thoughts to dwell on untruths. Read verses 1–10 to understand his circumstances. Now read verse 12. What did God think of Gideon?

_____

_____

_____

How would you contrast this with Gideon's thoughts about himself (see verses 13, 15)?

_____

_____

_____

Gideon considered himself a weakling and a nobody. What empowered him to become a mighty warrior (see verses 12, 16, 22)?

_____

_____

_____

_____

The Lord saw Gideon for who he could be if he lived from the truth of God's presence in his life. When Gideon, the fearful farmer, began to align his thoughts with truth, he became a fearless fighter. The disciples Peter and John understood this truth. They boldly performed miracles and preached the gospel in spite of arrest and imprisonment, and countless people responded. We might tend to put them on a spiritual pedestal and assume we could never live such dynamic Christian lives, but we need to think again. How are they described in Acts 4:13?

_____

_____

_____

_____

What was the secret to their strength (see verses 8, 13)?

_____

_____

_____

_____

The Holy Spirit is alive and well today. His role is to empower you for godly living. Read these verses from Romans 8 and identify His work on your behalf.

VERSE	HOW THE HOLY SPIRIT EMPOWERS YOU
2	
6	
11	
12-13	
16	
23	
26	

Which of these truths resonates with you? Why?

Satan hurls his best deceptive efforts at your mind so you will consider yourself weak and incapable. Reject these lies and live from the truth. The moment you placed your faith in Christ, the Holy Spirit took up residence in you and began His good work. Invite Him to fill, control, and empower you moment by moment.

Father God, I invite Your Holy Spirit to empower me. Make me the creative, courageous, strong person You designed me to be. Amen.

— DAY 6: REFLECTION AND APPLICATION

Lord God, oftentimes I feel like a loser. Change my mind, please, and teach me to see myself as You do. Amen.

I recently traveled to Nepal to train pastors and church leaders. One of those leaders was a nineteen-year-old woman who traveled six days by bus to attend the conference. Her effort spoke volumes to me about her desire to grow spiritually. Her eyes sparkled, and her face radiated joy. At one point, the conference director motioned to her to join us in conversation. "Tell Grace your story," he said. "Tell her how Jesus changed your life."

This gal—we'll call her Tara—spoke with confidence and enthusiasm. As one of ten children in her family, she had borne the brunt of her brothers' ridicule her entire life. "You're ugly," they had yelled. "You're no good. No man will ever want you for a wife." The abuse worsened after the village pastor told her about Jesus and she became a Christian.

The pastor knew of a Bible training school in Kathmandu. He contacted the school's director, told him about Tara's situation, and received an invitation for her to attend the four-month course.

"When Tara arrived at the center," the director said, "I took one look at her and thought I'd made a terrible mistake. She knew nothing about personal hygiene, couldn't look anyone in the eye, and was too shy to talk. But Jesus transformed her into this beautiful woman standing here today."

"How did He do that?" I asked.

"I'd grown to believe the lies my brothers spoke," said Tara. "I thought I was ugly. I believed I was dirty trash. But spending time in God's Word every day helped me understand that I was precious and loved. I learned that God delights in me and has made me His ambassador. Every morning I looked in the mirror and spoke truth over myself: 'You are beautiful. You are precious. You are God's handiwork. He loves you.' These words breathed life into me."

The director nodded and smiled. "Tara transformed within two months," he said.

Tara's family scarcely recognized her when she returned to the village. She boldly told them about Jesus, and everyone—including her brothers—chose to follow Him.

Not everyone in the village was as accepting. One neighbor tried to kill her using a razor-sharp knife. Tara escaped death, but a deep gash on her foot left her with a permanent scar and slight limp. One of her brothers threatened to retaliate against the neighbor, but Tara stopped him. "Leave her alone," she said. "I forgive her."

Every day, Tara hikes the terraced hills surrounding her village. Her passion for Jesus compels her to take the good news of salvation to men and women far and wide. She is living from the truth that God is crazy in love with her. She is living proof of the power of truth to set us free.

Almighty God, flood my mind with fresh understanding of Your love for me and transform me as You wish. Amen.

— DAY 7: REFLECTION AND APPLICATION

Lord God, thank You for speaking truth to me in various ways. Tune my ear to hear Your voice above those that speak lies. Amen.

The words other people speak into our lives and the manner in which they treat us shape the way we view ourselves. Affirmation and positive attention inspires us and instills courage and confidence in us. Constant criticism and negative attention, on the other hand, can discourage us, mar us, and put a big splat on the canvas of our self-worth for life.

That sounds grim. But wait—there's good news! Did you notice the wording in the previous sentence? The negative can affect us in less-than-favorable ways, but it doesn't have to. The secret to rising above lies in the thoughts we habitually entertain about Whose we are.

David's story provides a good example. He was a teenage shepherd, responsible for his dad's flocks. One day, his father told him to take a care package to his three oldest brothers, who were soldiers in King Saul's army. When he arrived, he witnessed the Philistine giant Goliath taunt and terrorize the Israelite army.

David's curiosity prompted him to ask questions about the situation, which annoyed his older brother Eliab. Read 1 Samuel 17:28–29. How would you describe Eliab's outburst? How might his words have left a splat on the canvas of David's self-worth?

___

How did David respond to Eliab?

___

King Saul heard about the shepherd boy's tenacity and sent for him. Read verse 33. How would you describe his response to David?

___

Read verses 34–37. Where did David's confidence lie?

___

MYplace O BIBLE STUDY

Compare verse 26 with verse 36. How did David view God? How did his thoughts about God affect his behavior?

_____

_____

_____

Saul tried to convince David to wear his armor (see verse 38). How might David have interpreted Saul's actions apart from his strong sense of belonging to the living God?

_____

_____

_____

Enter Goliath (see verses 41–44). Imagine being cursed by a nine-foot giant whose sole mission was to kill you. Put yourself in David's sandals. How might you have felt?

_____

_____

_____

Read verses 45-47. How did David respond? Again, from where did his courage come?

_____

_____

_____

David's courage didn't suddenly appear that day. He was ready for the battle because he had developed a meaningful relationship with the living God behind the scenes. He understood who God was because he had experienced His power. He also understood this same God cradled him in His hands. Other people's opinions of him didn't faze him. He knew God valued him, and that's what mattered most. How have other people's words and actions shaped your thoughts about your worth negatively and positively?

_____

_____

_____

How might your words and actions be shaping someone else's thoughts about his or her worth?

_____

_____

_____

Resolve to speak life into others' lives. Write a prayer asking God to empower you to do this.

_____

_____

_____

Almighty God, I choose to believe You value me. Thank You for the freedom that truth brings. Amen.

WEEK SIX: MOVING FROM FEAR TO FREEDOM

SCRIPTURE MEMORY VERSE

*I sought the L*ORD*, and he answered me; he delivered me from all my fears. Those who look to him are radiant; their faces are never covered with shame.*

Psalm 34:4–5

Fear is no stranger to me or the rest of mankind. Humanly speaking, every day brings more reason to fear what tomorrow might bring. Threats of nuclear warfare, terrorist attacks, and mass shootings top the list. Add to that the personal issues with which we all struggle—the fear of inadequacy, of failure, and for our loved ones' well-being. And, for most of us, the fear of stepping on a weight scale.

Even Adam and Eve dealt with fear: "Then the man and his wife heard the sound of the Lord God as he was walking in the garden in the cool of the day, and they hid from the Lord God among the trees of the garden. But the Lord God called to the man, 'Where are you?' He answered, 'I heard you in the garden, and I was afraid because I was naked; so I hid'" (Genesis 3:8–10).

God never intended for us to live in fear. But Adam and Eve started it, and we've been hiding ever since. We fear what others think about us, so we hide behind the mask of "I've got it all together." We fear others' discovering our hidden wounds, so we hide behind a façade of wholeness. We fear failure in a new endeavor, so we hide behind excuses for not taking the first step. I recently read an article that suggested we fear face-to-face and phone conversations, so we text instead. (Okay, that one strikes too close to home.)

Sometimes, fear shows up unexpectedly and hijacks us mentally, emotionally, and even spiritually. We can scarcely breathe, let alone think rationally. Other times, it sneaks in undetected and takes up residence in our minds before we realize what has happened. It drives the decisions we make and the manner in which we engage with people, but we don't recognize it.

Much of our fear begins in our minds. When I was a little girl, I thought monsters were real. I came to believe they lived in our basement and wanted to do me harm.

Fear nearly devoured me every time my mother told me to fetch something from downstairs, and my behavior reflected it. I fairly flew up those stairs after retrieving potatoes or canned peaches. I never told Mom how I felt because—you guessed it—I was afraid she would think I was a coward.

The Bible references fear 366 times. That's one for every day of the calendar with an extra for leap year. It seems God knows fear is a big deal for mankind, and He wants to equip us with the truth needed to set us free from its grip.

This week, we will examine several common fears and the role our thoughts play in their development. Best of all, we will discover the truth about how to change our minds so living in peace becomes our reality.

—— DAY 1: WHO, ME?

Dear Father, thank You for promising to equip me for whatever You call me to do. I choose to trust and not be afraid, even though I feel inadequate for the task. Amen.

In the introduction to Week 6, I mentioned my fear of writing a chapter book in obedience to God's prompting. I thought I lacked the needed skills to get the job done and that saying yes would only confirm my suspicions. Why set myself up for failure? Mine was a classic case of the fear of inadequacy. Moses felt the same way when God called him to lead a rescue mission. Read Exodus 3:7–11. Some Bible scholars believe the exodus involved approximately 2.4 million people! How did Moses respond (see verse 11)?

_____

_____

_____

_____

Note God's next words to Moses: "_____"
(verse 12). What's the significance of this declaration at this point in the
conversation?

_____

_____

_____

Perhaps God's assurance was meant to refocus Moses' thoughts. If so, it fell on
deaf ears. What was Moses' next argument (see verse 13)? Where was his focus?

_____

_____

_____

Read verses 14–22. List some of the words and phrases that show God's role in
this mission. With this in mind, why was Moses still afraid?

_____

_____

_____

Read Exodus 4:1–10. God gave Moses step-by-step instructions and
demonstrations of His power, but Moses only grew more desperate. What
excuse did he give in verse 10?

_____

_____

_____

Can you relate? I can. Truth be told, I almost refused to register for an online First Place for Health group because accountability scared me. I worried what would happen if I set a weight goal and failed to achieve it. What arguments and excuses have you used when God has prompted you to do something that felt much too big for you to handle?

_____

_____

_____

_____

What was God's response to Moses (see verse 11)? What command did He give? What promises did He give immediately after issuing the command (see verse 12)?

_____

_____

_____

_____

Moses attempted one last plea (see verse 13). How did God respond (see verse 14)? What do you suppose the reason was for God's anger?

_____

_____

_____

_____

Henry Blackaby says, "Anytime God leads you to do something that has God-sized dimensions, you will face a crisis of belief. When you face a crisis of belief, what you do next reveals what you really believe about God."[1] Based on Moses's behavior, what did he believe to be true about God?

_____

_____

_____

Overcoming the fear of inadequacy requires knowing the truth about who God is and what He will do for us. Read the following verses, and then write your answers in the appropriate boxes.

VERSE	TRUTH ABOUT GOD	TRUTH ABOUT WHAT GOD DOES FOR US
Psalm 18:28-36		
Psalm 23:1-3		
Psalm 25:4-5		
Psalm 84:11		
Psalm 95:3-7		

What truth from the above exercise is especially meaningful to you? How can you apply this truth to your wellness journey?

_____

_____

_____

You might feel inadequate for the task, but rest assured that God is more than able to help you succeed.

> *Father, please help me keep my focus on Your adequacy, not my inadequacies. Amen.*

— DAY 2: WILL THEY BE OKAY?

Father, thank You for loving those I love far more than I ever could. Teach me to trust You with their care. Amen.

Before I wrote *Moving from Fear to Freedom*, I asked approximately 350 women aged nineteen to eighty to identify the fears with which they struggled. Fear for their kids' well-being scored twice as high as the next item on the list.[2] Most of us can relate, but we also fear for extended family members and dear friends. Whatever the relationship, we often feel what Aristotle called "the pain that arises from the anticipation of evil." That anticipation of evil revolves around the thoughts we entertain. What fearful thoughts do you have for a loved one?

_____

_____

_____

_____

Fear, if left unchecked, will negatively affect you. How has it affected you personally? Be honest. Has it led you down the path of stress-related eating?

_____

_____

_____

_____

Fear can keep us awake at night and make us physically ill. It can cause us to turn to food, alcohol, or drugs to help cope. It turns us into control freaks. I suggest we say, "Enough!" and take action to deal with it appropriately. Read 1 Peter 5:7–8. Write verse 7 and circle key words.

_____

_____

_____

_____

Let's study those key words. **Cast**—the original Greek term denotes flinging or hurling an excess weight with force. The same word is used in Luke 19:35 when the disciples flung their garments on the donkey's back. Likewise, we fling our excess weight—our fears—onto Someone's back because it's too heavy for us to bear.

All—means what it says. We surrender all, not some, of our fears.

Anxiety—anything that causes hardship, difficulty, or trouble.

Him—Almighty God, the Strong One who never fails.

Cares—the original Greek term means "to be concerned, thoughtful, aware, or to give painful and meticulous attention to."[3] God is well aware of the issue that is troubling you. It is no surprise to Him.

WEEK SIX MOVING FROM FEAR TO FREEDOM

You—you, my friend, are the focus of God's undivided attention. He knows your concerns and wants to carry them for you. Will you release your loved ones to Him? Fill in the blanks for verse 8:

Be _____ and of _____ . Your enemy _____ prowls around like a roaring lion looking for someone to _____ .

To be alert means to be on constant guard so an enemy cannot gain entry into your life or residence. Who is the enemy wanting access to your life? How has he used fear as a tactic?

_____

_____

_____

_____

_____

We are to be on constant vigil. What does that say about the enemy's persistence?

_____

_____

_____

_____

The enemy's goal is to devour you, and he might try to do that through food-related issues. Fight back with the sword of truth. Speak 1 Peter 5:7 and other promises aloud. Stand firm against the enemy and expect God to help.

Almighty God, I surrender my anxieties and my loved ones to Your care. Grant me peace. Amen.

— DAY 3: WHEN STORMS BLOW

Jesus, teach me to recall truth when tough stuff happens. Fill me with peace rather than panic. Amen.

Life being what it is, you will experience storms at times: the loss of a loved one or possessions, unemployment, chronic illness, divorce, a crippling accident, or a significant transition. Sometimes you will see the winds coming, like a sailor observing the telltale ripples on the water's surface. But oftentimes these storms will sweep in without a moment's notice. What thoughts fill your mind when a storm strikes?

_____

_____

_____

_____

The thoughts you habitually entertain will determine your beliefs and behaviors. Therefore, it matters a great deal to fill your mind with truth. Without truth and the hope it brings, you will turn to food and other things to numb your stress. Read Isaiah 43:1–5. What command does God give you? What truths enable you to obey this command (see verse 1)?

_____

_____

_____

_____

_____

In verse 2, God gives a promise that He repeats in verse 5. What is it? What difference should it make for you?

_____

_____

_____

_____

Read Joshua 1:6–9. God spoke these words to Joshua when He appointed him to be leader of the Israelites in Moses's place. Perhaps this massive transition filled Joshua's mind with fear and uncertainty and God wanted to reassure him that everything would be okay. What command did God issue three times (see verses 6, 7, 9)? What promise did He make?

_____

_____

_____

_____

What three things did God tell Joshua to do with His Word? What did God promise would be the outcome if he obeyed (see verse 8)?

_____

_____

_____

_____

God promised success in Joshua's new role if he spoke the truth, meditated on it, and obeyed it. Interestingly, scientific research shows that meditation shrinks the amygdala, the part of the brain that governs stress and fear responses. As the amygdala shrinks, we naturally feel more at peace.[4] Meditating on God's truth—mulling it over, pondering it—will help you weather tumult. Why is this so? Identify reasons other than shrinking the amygdala.

___

Read John 14:27. Jesus spoke these words to the disciples, knowing they would soon face the storm of His arrest and crucifixion. Their faith and courage would be tested to the max. What command did He give to them? What promise did He give?

___

Read Isaiah 26:3. How can you access that peace?

___

Fear is real. Even Jesus—the Prince of Peace—experienced it. Read Matthew 26:38–44. How did Jesus respond to fear? What does His example teach you?

_____

_____

_____

We often view storms negatively, but Jesus reframed them. Read Matthew 10:16–18. What are several opportunities that storms bring? What was a storm in your life that brought you unexpected opportunities or blessings?

_____

_____

_____

_____

Father, thank You for understanding our fears and gifting us with truth to deal with them appropriately. Amen.

— DAY 4: SAYING GOODBYE TO THE GHOSTS IN MY PAST

God, I'm not proud of my past. Sometimes I fear I've gone too far. Amen.

I interviewed a woman named Jan whose uncle—a church leader—sexually abused her for seventeen years. She never told a soul. After high school, she began a quest for true love. Her search lasted nearly twenty years and resulted in four divorces. She suffered nervous breakdowns, panic attacks, depression, and psychosomatic physical ailments.

MYplace O BIBLE STUDY

Jan had learned about prayer as a child, but she figured it wasn't worth the bother. She thought God couldn't possibly care about her after what she had done. She was afraid she was "too far gone." But then a friend asked her to a women's event, where the speaker invited the audience members to trust Jesus for salvation. Jan responded by raising her pointer finger under the tablecloth. *I'm so ashamed of myself*, she thought. *God, I know You don't want to associate with me, but do You see my finger? I'm trying to tell You that I need You.*

Jan feared her past labeled her "beyond hope." Read Luke 7:36–50. The woman in this story felt the same way. What was her reputation? What were her actions toward Jesus (see verses 37–38)?

_____

_____

_____

It would have been unusual for a woman of her profession to weep as she did. What do you think prompted that outburst of emotion (see verse 47)? How did Jesus respond to her?

_____

_____

_____

Jesus spoke words this woman needed to hear. What did He say (see verses 48–50)? What is the significance of His affirming her in public?

_____

_____

_____

WEEK SIX MOVING FROM FEAR TO FREEDOM

What is the significance of Jesus telling the woman to go in peace? What emotions had she likely known until that point in her life?

___

Wrong thinking about a painful past implies you are beyond the scope of God's redemption. Read Matthew 11:28 and Isaiah 55:1–3. What invitation does Jesus extend and to whom?

___

What promise does Jesus make to those who accept His invitation (see John 6:37)?

___

Misperception leads us to believe our sin stains us forever. Read 1 John 1:9, Psalm 103:12, and Isaiah 1:18. What does God do with our sins?

___

Wrong thinking leads us to believe God records our sins to use against us one day. Read Isaiah 43:25 and Hebrews 8:12. What does God actually do with our sins?

_____

_____

_____

As if that weren't enough, God makes us new. Read 2 Corinthians 5:17. What new attitudes and behaviors is God birthing in you?

_____

_____

_____

God desires to heal you and set you free from the fear of His rejection due to a painful past. He also wants to set you free from masking your pain with food and the bondage to which this leads. When you give Him your deepest pain and shame, He often transforms it into your most effective ministry for His glory. He did this for Jan, and He wants to do it for you. Read Isaiah 61:3. What shifts are happening in your thinking as a result of today's truth?

_____

_____

_____

Forgiving Father, I'm grateful for Your acceptance of me. Take my painful past and use it for Your glory. Amen.

— DAY 5: WHAT DOES THE FUTURE HOLD?

Lord, the future looks grim at times. Help me remember that I do not need to be afraid because You are already there. Amen.

If we could collect all our worrisome and fearful thoughts into one bundle, we would find about eight percent warrant our attention. Studies show that forty percent of the things we fear never happen, thirty percent have already happened (or are those over which we have no control), twelve percent involve health issues of no valid concern, and ten percent are irrelevant. Still, we allow our minds to take us to a place void of joy and peace, and then our behaviors follow. Bring on our favorite go-to stress foods!

Let's face it—the future is one big unknown over which we have little control. Now, that's a scary thought, but living scared isn't what God intends for us. He wants us to align our minds with truth so we can live with courage and confidence. Read Numbers 13:1–33. God had promised His people a good future. What was the spies' mission (see verses 2, 18–20)?

_____

_____

_____

What promise had God made (see verse 2)? How did the spies describe the land (see verse 27)?

_____

_____

_____

You would think the Israelites would have been eager to claim the land promised to them. But this intel group clearly held two perspectives. Compare the two viewpoints in verses 30–31. What thoughts caused the ten spies to spread discouraging reports? How did these thoughts determine their beliefs and behavior (see verses 28–29, 31–33)?

_____

_____

_____

_____

Read Numbers 14:1–4, 10. The report caused an instant chain reaction. What wrong thoughts filled the Israelites' minds?

_____

_____

_____

_____

What did these thoughts lead them to believe? How did those thoughts determine their behavior?

_____

_____

_____

_____

Read verses 6–9. Joshua and Caleb saw the same mission through eyes of faith. Write the phrases that show the Source of their courage.

_____

_____

_____

_____

In verse 9, Joshua and Caleb said "do not" three times. What were they cautioning the Israelites not to do? How would you explain the correlation between fear and disobedience?

_____

_____

_____

_____

Recall a situation when fear of the unknown led to your disobeying the Lord. Conversely, recall a time when you obeyed despite your fear. What did you learn? How did God honor you?

_____

_____

_____

_____

One thing of which we can be certain is that the future is uncertain. But here's hope God's truth is unshakeable. Match the following verses to their truth.

VERSE	TRUTH
Matthew 10:29–30	God brings good from every trial
Romans 8:28	God always keeps His promises
Hebrews 13:8	God cares about the details of our lives
Psalm 34:4	God frees us from our fears
Numbers 23:19	God remains the same always

Read Psalm 77. Contrast the tone of verses 1–9 with verses 12–20. What changed the writer's tone from lament to praise (see verses 11–12)? How does recalling God's faithfulness in the past bring courage for the future?

_____

_____

_____

_____

Choose the verse that means the most to you from the list above, write it out, and post it either on your fridge or snack cupboard door. Read it aloud when fear urges you to find peace in food rather than in God's promises and presence.

> *Almighty God, thank You for being my faithful and loving Savior forever and ever. Amen.*

— DAY 6: REFLECTION AND APPLICATION

Lord God, thank You for Your presence. Knowing I'm never alone changes everything for me. Amen.

My husband worked as a civil engineer for the first fourteen years of our marriage and traveled frequently for work. I stayed home with our three little ones.

I dreaded Gene's business trips. Fear of falling victim to a home invasion kept me awake every night in his absence. The "what-ifs" tormented me: What if someone breaks in? What if I can't defend myself? What if I can't protect the kids? I kept a bedroom lamp on all night because I thought seeing a perpetrator's face would help me later identify him for the police.

My fears were not unfounded. Someone had robbed our home one afternoon when I had taken the kids to the park, and the thief was never caught. We suspected the culprit was our next-door neighbor or one of his sketchy friends, and I worried that he might return when he knew Gene was away.

One night, my thoughts ran rampant as bedtime approached. I had grown to hate the paralyzing effect of these thoughts, and I felt tired of being tired from staying awake so many hours every night. You could say I had reached a point of desperation.

I locked the doors, crawled into bed, and reached for my Bible. For no particular reason, I turned to Psalm 127:1–2 and read, "Unless the Lord builds a house, the work of the builders is useless. Unless the Lord protects a city, guarding it with sentries will do no good. It is useless for you to work so hard from early morning until late at night, anxiously working for food to eat; for God gives rest to his loved ones" (NLT).

Those words gave me a spiritual "aha" moment. Fearful thinking had robbed me of God's rest in more ways than one. Each time Gene packed his suitcase, I had told myself that I would be alone with the kids—but that was a lie. As time passed, I had believed the lies were true, and my behavior reflected my beliefs.

The truth was that I was never alone. God had promised time and time again that He would never leave me or forsake me. His presence lived in me and permeated my home. Why, then, did I need to place my trust for protection in the lamp on my nightstand and my hoped-for ability to remember an assailant's face?

I had worked hard in anticipation of a home invasion when God intended for me to experience rest. God's presence is a truth that stands forever for those who love Him, but fearful thinking often overshadows it.

Here's a simple but profound exercise I've found helpful to keep my thoughts aligned with His. Complete the following sentence: "Your presence is with me, therefore _____." One of my frequent answers is, "Therefore, I will trust and not be afraid." Finish the sentence with at least five truth declarations.

_____

_____

_____

_____

_____

_____

_____

_____

_____

_____

God, thank You for Your presence. It calms my fears and gives me rest. Amen.

— DAY 7: REFLECTION AND APPLICATION

Almighty God, thank You for promising to deliver me from my fears. You alone are my source of hope and strength in the face of life's tough stuff. Amen.

When you're in the middle of really tough stuff, your mind will automatically migrate toward your circumstances. But allowing your thoughts to dwell there guarantees a win for anxiety and fear, because you will begin to presume outcomes to what-ifs.

Have you ever caught yourself engaging in a monologue sounding something like this? "What if I lose my job? Then I'll have to find another one. But what if I can't? Then I won't be able to pay the bills. What if I can't pay the rent? Then I'll end up on the street."

I once caught myself in a conversation about my husband's mortality. We were sitting on our favorite loveseat—he was watching a baseball game on TV, and I was on Facebook. I glanced at him and thought, *I'm so lucky. I couldn't have wished for a better husband.*

A nanosecond later, I thought, *Life would be so different without him. What would I do if he suddenly died? I can't even balance a checkbook or change a tire. Oh, no—I'm in big trouble.* My eyes filled with tears as I began thinking about how to celebrate his life and how to break the news to our kids that their dad had passed away.

Thankfully, the Holy Spirit intervened before I reached for the phone. And thankfully, God knows our human foibles. He is well aware of our natural bent towards fear, so He has given us the remedy. Read Psalm 34:1–3, the verses immediately preceding this week's memory verse. What does the writer commit to doing constantly and at all times?

_____

_____

_____

How would you define the word *extol*?

_____

_____

_____

How would you define the word *praise*?

_____

_____

_____

It's no coincidence that praise is the focus immediately prior to the declaration that God delivers you from your fears. How does practicing praise at all times give you the victory over fear's destructive force?

_____

_____

_____

Wrong thinking says God is an egomaniac, a divine sponge soaking up His creation's adoration. The truth says He's our Creator. He wove us in our mother's womb and understands how our mind and body functions best. He knows the negative impact of fear and the power of praise to counteract it. Therefore, He commands us to focus our thoughts on His character and to verbalize the truth about who He is.

Earlier in this study, you learned that obedience to the Lord proves your love for Him. And so, here's an opportunity to demonstrate your love. Begin practicing praise this moment.

WEEK SIX MOVING FROM FEAR TO FREEDOM

Think of one characteristic of God that is especially meaningful in your current challenge and write a prayer of praise to Him within the context of your circumstances.

_____

_____

_____

_____

_____

Heavenly Father, I praise You for Your wisdom and kindness. Thank You for lavishing them on me through Your command to praise at all times. Give me a heart to obey even when it's hard, and the power to do it. Amen.

WEEK SEVEN: KEEPING FIRST THINGS FIRST

SCRIPTURE MEMORY VERSE
But seek first his kingdom and his righteousness, and all these things will be given to you as well.

Matthew 6:33

Every person sets priorities, whether intentionally or not. Our thoughts determine the ones we choose, and our behavior reveals them. For instance, a person who longs to become an accomplished musician takes private lessons and perhaps pursues a musical degree. He or she practices every day. The person may have to say no to doing other activities, but he or she doesn't mind because music is the priority.

The son of a close friend of mine chose to pursue a career in real estate. He attended classes, did his homework, and studied for the exam. He failed it, but nothing could deter him from seeing his dream fulfilled. He repeated the course, pouring his heart and soul into his studies, and wrote the exam again. This time he passed with an impressive score. Why? Because he made his future a priority. His behavior proved it.

You've certainly thought about making changes in your overall well-being. You bought this study, scheduled time to attend a group meeting, and committed to showing up every week, barring the unexpected. You're making your health a priority. Your behavior says so. Bravo! Your thoughts have played a vital role in determining your priorities, and your actions have followed. A healthy mind produces healthy outcomes.

Sadly, the opposite is also true. For example, I've witnessed the breakdown of several friends' marriages. In each case, their spouses thought extra-marital affairs were okay. Their thoughts led to beliefs that someone other than their wives could increase their happiness. They gave personal pleasure higher priority than integrity and their family's welfare, and their behavior proved it.

God designed us and knows the power our minds have over the direction our lives take. He wants to protect us from the pain that negative or sinful behaviors inflict on us. That's why He instructs us to seek His kingdom and righteousness above all else. When we align our thoughts with His, everything else falls into place.

God also knows our tendency to worry and fear. Will we have enough money to pay the mortgage and feed our family? Will we have enough to buy clothes and pay medical expenses? If we come up short at month's end, what will we do about it?

Our thoughts can lead us down a path that looks okay and feels right, but this path is not what it seems. This path leads to the belief that God isn't big enough to supply our needs. It leads to the belief that we must assume full responsibility, doing whatever it takes to provide for ourselves and our families—even if it means sacrificing relationships with others and the Lord.

God commands us to make Him our top priority because He loves us. He wants us to flourish. Giving Him first place in our affections, and then aligning other priorities with His, is the key. With this in mind, let's explore what the Bible teaches about these priorities so we can understand and personalize them.

— DAY 1: THE FIRST AND GREATEST COMMANDMENT

Lord God, You deserve first place in my life because of who You are and what You've done for me. Teach me to make You my utmost priority. Amen.

So many voices clamor for importance in our lives. Business professionals tell us that we must focus on social networking to achieve success. Marriage and family experts tell us to make our spouse and children a priority. Wellness gurus tell us to invest in self-care. To whom should we listen? In the midst of the plethora of demands, only one thing urgently deserves our attention, because it determines everything about us. Read Luke 10:38–42. What was Mary doing?

_____

_____

_____

What was Martha doing? What was her mental and emotional state?

_____

_____

_____

What did Jesus say to Martha (see verses 41–42)? What is the one thing that matters most?

_____

_____

_____

Martha meant well, but she misplaced her priorities. I've done the same thing. I used to think that, as a good Christian woman, I should teach Sunday school, lead a weekly kids' program at church, be on the worship team, and support my husband's ministry—all while homeschooling my three children.

I worked hard to fulfill those self-imposed expectations. Trouble was, I served God to the neglect of spending time in His presence. Within two years, I grew frustrated rather than fulfilled, and I suffered burnout. In retrospect, my service for God wasn't motivated by love. I was seeking to fill emotional needs. I craved others' affirmation and said yes to every request because I feared disappointing someone with a no. I stayed busy, afraid to stop and sit in quiet, lest the Holy Spirit show me painful areas in my life that needed change.

Perhaps you can relate. Has serving God taken priority over friendship with Him in your life? If so, in what ways?

_____

_____

_____

What needs to change to make your love relationship with God your utmost priority? What is one action you can take to align your priorities with His?

_____

_____

_____

Read Exodus 20:1–6. What command does God issue in verses 3–4?

_____

_____

_____

Food certainly can become an idol. Are you quick to run to the refrigerator instead of to God? Do you think food can give you something God cannot? Other gods might include money, a title or position, or material goods. Or you might idolize your children, your career, or a hobby. Anything you love more than the Lord is a lesser god. How does God feel about sharing your affection with other gods (see verse 5)?

_____

_____

_____

God is adamant that you obey this command, because who you become flows from your priorities. When you love Him more than anything or anyone else, it assures that you will flourish mentally, emotionally, spiritually, and physically. Loving lesser gods will put you in bondage to them, but loving God first and foremost secures your freedom.

Father, thank You for showing me that abundant life comes from loving You and obeying Your commands. You are my everything. Amen.

— DAY 2: LOVE OTHERS

Father God, teach me to see others through Your eyes. Make me a channel through which You can love others unconditionally. Amen.

Read Matthew 22:37–39 and Mark 12:30–31. The first and greatest command is to _____ . What is the second command?

_____

_____

_____

It's easy to assume the command to love God sits at a higher level than loving others. But this is a misperception. Ponder the significance of the words "the second is like it" (Matthew 22:39). What do these words tell you about these commands?

_____

_____

_____

Loving God and loving others are of equal significance. Obeying the first transforms your thoughts, beliefs, and behaviors so you are better able to obey the second. Obeying the second provides visible evidence that you are obeying the first. You can't have one without the other. Read Matthew 5:16. How does this principle apply to these commands?

_____

_____

_____

Now read Matthew 22:40. On what do all other commands and the demands of the prophets depend? What does this indicate about their significance?

_____

_____

_____

_____

_____

Everything about the Bible, from start to finish, is about humans loving God and each other. The world would look much different if all people aligned their thoughts regarding these two commandments with God's thoughts! Obviously, God considers demonstrating love to other people a top priority. Unfortunately, our human bent doesn't always agree. Read Luke 10:25–37. This story explains why our thoughts differ from God's in the context of loving others. What are the three responses to the man had been left to die (see verses 31–33)?

_____

_____

_____

_____

The first two men looked upon the victim and turned away because they didn't see him as worthy of their time and attention. How sad! The third man looked as well, but he saw the man through God's eyes. Having God's perspective compelled him to action.

It's easy to give our personal prejudices and schedules priority over people. I'm guilty of this, but God is changing me. I regularly pray, "Father, help me see other people through Your eyes." I don't want to just look upon other people and turn away; I want to see them as God does—as individuals highly valued—and then demonstrate love as the Holy Spirit leads me.

Twice in the past two weeks, I've crossed paths with homeless men. Rather than looking on them and turning away, I felt compassion and was moved to give them several pieces of fresh fruit I had purchased just a few minutes before. What is one simple action you can take to show love to someone who is hurting?

___

___

___

God doesn't just "look upon" people; He sees their needs and responds. Read Genesis 16:1–13. What were Hagar's needs? How would you describe her encounter with God?

___

___

What did Hagar name Him (see verse 13)? How did experiencing His love and knowing that He saw her needs change her?

___

___

___

Recall a personal experience when you realized God saw you and loved you. How did this change you?

___

___

___

Father God, thank You for seeing me and responding to my needs. Help me to see others through Your eyes and be a willing vessel through which You demonstrate love. Amen.

— DAY 3: PURSUE HOLINESS

Lord, I long to become more like You, but my humanity keeps getting in the way. I need Your help! Amen.

Some people think that being a Christian means all their past, present, and future sins are forgiven, so they can now live as they please. But how does this belief compare to the truth? Read 1 Thessalonians 4:7. In this passage, Paul says that God has called you to live a life of _____ . How does being holy differ from being a good person?

_____

_____

_____

_____

_____

How would you define the word *holiness*?

_____

_____

_____

_____

The best definition of holiness I've read to date is from J.C. Ryle: "Holiness is the habit of being of one mind with God, according as we find His mind described in Scripture. It is the habit of agreeing in God's judgment, hating what He hates, loving what He loves, and measuring everything in this world by the standard of His Word."[1] Read 1 Peter 1:13–16. How would you respond to a person who asked, "Why be holy because God is holy"?

_____

_____

_____

We are God's ambassadors to a hurting, watching world. We represent Him most accurately when we think the way He does, because our attitudes and behavior will then reflect His character and point others to Jesus. Holy living also ensures we make wise choices. We behave with integrity, respond well to hardships, respect others who are different than us or are difficult to love, and so forth.

All said, living a holy life protects us from self-inflicted, avoidable heartache. It even plays a vital role in our efforts to achieve better health. For me, understanding gluttony as sin transformed my way of thinking about my appetite and food. I wanted to please the Lord, which meant turning away from the sin of overeating. Practicing holiness in this regard helped me lose more than sixty pounds and keep it off.

The quote above from J.C. Ryle states that "holiness is the habit of being of one mind with God." Developing any habit requires time and intentionality. We play a role, but God has also given us a Helper to teach us and guide us. Read John 14:16–17. Who is this Helper? Where does He live?

_____

_____

_____

_____

Read Romans 8:12–14. Where does following your sinful nature lead?

_____

_____

_____

What happens if you cooperate with the Spirit?

_____

_____

_____

Read Galatians 5:16–18. Your old sinful nature wages constant battle with your new life in the Holy Spirit. Complete the chart with three personal examples of the battles you face.

MY OLD NATURE SAYS...	THE HOLY SPIRIT WANTS...

The more you surrender to the Holy Spirit, the more He takes control of your life and transforms you. It is a sweet partnership that results in the holiness God desires. Read Galatians 5:22–23. What is the evidence of His work in you?

_____

_____

_____

Read Galatians 5:24–25. How do these verses strengthen your resolve in your pursuit of holiness?

_____

_____

_____

Dear Father, thank You for sending Your Holy Spirit to create in me the holiness You desire. I am free and fully alive in Christ. Amen.

— DAY 4: TIME

Lord, my life is only a breath compared to Your eternity. Teach me to view time as You do. Amen.

In the introduction to this week's lesson, I wrote, "Our thoughts can lead us down a path that looks okay and feels right, but this path is not what it seems." Consider this statement in the context of time. One week consists of 168 hours. A full-time job generally takes up forty hours. Sleeping requires about forty-nine. Personal care and food preparation usually takes three hours. That leaves fifty-eight hours for friends and family, exercise, volunteering, church-related activities, hobbies, and house maintenance. Sounds doable, right?

It's totally doable—until our human nature gets in the way. A recent Neilson report found the average American adult spends more than fifty hours each week engaged in media gadgets for entertainment purposes. How much time is then left for meaningful activities? Nearly none.[2] Pastor Chip Ingram says, "We must recognize how the evil one is working in this world and take a firm stance against him. It means we take careful thought concerning what we put in our minds—what we listen to, what we watch, and how we use our time."[3]

Read John 10:10. The enemy of your soul seeks to _____ , _____ , and _____ you. He will target your mind with misperceptions related to every area of your life, including the need to spend time caring for your body. A neighbor who knew I walked two miles a day once said, "Why do you waste your time doing this?" His job required a ton of activity, but mine meant sitting at a desk all day. The enemy could have used this remark to derail me, but thankfully I recognized it as faulty thinking about intentional exercise.

Sadly, Satan later used a different thought to gain a destructive foothold: *I don't have time to exercise now. I'll do it in a few hours.* Trouble was, I still felt too busy a few hours later. Procrastination is a form of faulty thinking about time. Within the context of your physical well-being, that mindset can reap negative consequences. What are a couple of lies that you have believed in regard to time and your physical well-being?

_____

_____

_____

Contrast those lies with the truth. What will be the outcome if you live from those lies?

_____

_____

_____

What will be the outcome if you live from the truth?

_____

_____

_____

Read Job 14:1–2 and compare with Psalm 90:5–6 and 102:11. You might assume you will live seventy-five or eighty years on this earth. That sounds like a long time, but with what does the Bible compare your lifespan?

_____

_____

_____

Read Isaiah 40:6–8. What is transient and fleeting? What lasts forever?

_____

_____

_____

Missionary C.T. Studd said, "Only one life, 'twill soon be past; only what's done for Christ will last."[4] This mindset has transformed my willingness to prioritize time for self-care. For me, my faulty thinking about spending time exercising resulted in obesity, chronic pain, and loss of mobility. Those consequences, in turn, limited my ability to invest in people's souls and God's kingdom. Living from the truth has set me free to live long and strong for Jesus, for which I am grateful. How are health-related issues hindering you from living long and strong for Jesus? What is one action you could take today to turn that around?

_____

_____

_____

Read Psalm 39:4–7, 13. How can you ensure right thinking about the way you spend your time?

_____

_____

_____

Lord, thank You for the gift of time. Help me value it and use it as You desire. Amen.

— DAY 5: MONEY

Father, living in a physical world means I need money and material possessions. Please help me think about these things as you do. Amen.

My husband and I are career missionaries. Our first house was perched on a Nepalese hillside. It was built of mud and rock with a thatch roof and had no electricity, running water, or indoor plumbing. It measured three giant steps wide and six giant steps long, with an upstairs sleeping area barely big enough to hold the foam mattress on which we slept.

In that place of owning next to nothing, God began teaching me to trust Him as my provider. I was a slow learner. The intensity of these lessons increased as our family grew and our ministry locations changed. To say my thinking differed from God's is an understatement. Read Exodus 20:2–3. What does making money an idol look like in your life?

_____

_____

_____

Read Matthew 6:24. I elevated our monthly paycheck to god status by considering it, rather than the Lord, as our source of provision. The result was that my stomach knotted in fear every payday morning for years. I worried, *What if the check isn't enough?* God used Scripture to renew my mind. Read Matthew 6:25–34. What (or who) is our source of provision? What is the truth about God's care for us (see verses 32–33)?

_____

_____

_____

_____

What is the promise? What is the condition (see verse 33)?

_____

_____

_____

God wants His kingdom—not finances—to be your primary concern. He expects you to be wise and responsible in money matters, but He doesn't want them to become your idol. Trusting in money for security only leads to fear-based behaviors. You might get a job that leaves you no time for higher priorities. You may start withholding donations to people or ministries that need them. You might lose sleep, literally worry yourself sick, or fall into stress-based overeating. You are so busy working and worrying that exercise is the last thing on your mind.

God has given you money to use as a tool, not to hold you in bondage. Your attitude toward it depends directly on the depth of your understanding of His character. What is your usual response when financial issues cause you stress?

___

Read Psalm 23:1. How does this verse describe the Lord? What are some characteristics of a good shepherd? What difference does God being a shepherd make in your life?

___

Read Psalm 37:16–19. What does this passage teach about Kingdom values? What promises does God give to those who love Him?

_____

_____

_____

Meditating on God's commands, promises, and character completely changed my mind about money. Making Proverbs 30:7–9 my prayer has also helped. Read these verses. What lies have you believed about finances and possessions?

_____

_____

_____

How have those lies influenced your behaviors and priorities?

_____

_____

_____

What change needs to take place to align your thoughts with truth?

_____

_____

_____

Father, thank You for knowing my needs. I rest in Your care. Amen.

— DAY 6: REFLECTION AND APPLICATION

Heavenly Father, thank You for giving me everything I need for victorious living. Help me to apply Your truth so I become more like Christ. Amen.

My youngest daughter, Kim, and the love of her life, David, got engaged four months after they met. They married five weeks later. My entire life shifted to ensure my daughter's wedding day would be special. I canceled appointments and an overseas trip to plan, shop, run errands, and be available to help in any way needed. The wedding took top priority for thirty-five days.

Jesus said, "Where your treasure is, there your heart will be also" (Luke 12:34). That summer, my treasure was my daughter, and I invested my energy, time, and resources into supporting her and David as they prepared to celebrate marriage. This treasure principle holds true in every area of our lives—our relationships, work, leisure, home, finances, health, and more. Whatever we hold near and dear becomes our focus. We willingly invest ourselves and rearrange our lives to accommodate what we value.

This principle holds true when comes to our spiritual well-being. If we consider a vibrant relationship with God important, then we do whatever is necessary to promote it. For me, this means scheduling daily quiet time with Jesus. I also participate in an online First Place for Health Bible study, attend a church with solid Bible teaching, meet with friends to pray for our kids every week, listen to praise and worship music, memorize the Word, and train my mind to identify and reject thoughts opposed to God's truth.

Our behaviors reveal our priorities. So, how do your behaviors—both public and private—reflect your priorities within the context of spiritual wellness? Have you allowed other treasures to assume priority over your spiritual well-being? If so, name them.

_____

_____

_____

What is one change you can make now to place these priorities where they belong?

_____

_____

_____

_____

Now think in terms of your physical well-being. I've learned the hard way to treasure my body and make my health a priority, and now I rise at 5:30 AM to visit the gym four times weekly. I make wise food choices, track my food intake, practice self-control when I'm tempted to overeat, and make myself accountable to my First Place for Health group leader.

Making these changes felt burdensome at first, but now I view them as good habits that will enable me to live long and strong for Jesus. Prioritizing my health has eliminated chronic pain and helped me achieve optimum weight. I never want to regress. And so, again, how do your behaviors—both public and private—reflect your priority in terms of health?

_____

_____

_____

_____

Have you allowed other treasures to assume priority over your physical well-being? If so, name them.

_____

_____

_____

_____

What is one change you can make now to place these priorities where they belong?

_____

_____

_____

_____

Lord, help me make Your values my priority. Give me the self-discipline needed to live intentionally. Thank You in advance. Amen.

— DAY 7: REFLECTION AND APPLICATION

Lord, thank You for loving me so well. Teach me how to love You in return, for You deserve my best. Amen.

C.S. Lewis said, "Put first things first and we get second things thrown in; put second things first and we lose both first and second things."[5] His words mirror the truth found in this week's memory verse: when we make Kingdom matters our priority, everything else falls into place. Write this week's verse by memory.

_____

_____

_____

_____

_____

_____

On Day 1, we talked about misplacing our Kingdom priorities. Putting service for God above our friendship with Him sets us on the infamous path to which I've referred several times—the one that looks okay and feels right, but it's really not. This path leads us to a place of relying on our own wisdom and strength instead of God's.

Eventually, this path also leads us to experience negative outcomes. We fall into pride about our accomplishments or become discouraged over the lack thereof. We turn into a human bulldozer and roll over people to achieve a desired outcome. We fear trusting others to help us, so we do the work ourselves and end up feeling stressed and underappreciated. We serve with the wrong motives, hoping to earn a few accolades or make a good impression. We lose our joy and peace and question whether serving God is worth the effort.

I've experienced all of the above. Focusing more on serving Jesus than on being His friend caused me to suffer burnout. Recovery took about two years and meant stepping back to put first things first again. I became intentional about spending undisturbed quiet time with the Lord early every morning, reading my Bible and journaling, and He began to create in me an insatiable appetite to know Him. The more I sought Him, the more He captivated me with His love. And when I began to understand the depth of His love for me, everything else fell into place.

Here are some verses that helped me understand God's desire for first place in my life. Read them and note both God's commands and His promises.

SITUATION:	GOD'S COMMANDS:	GOD'S PROMISES:
Deuteronomy 4:29		
1 Chronicles 28:9		
2 Chronicles 16:9		

SITUATION:	GOD'S COMMANDS:	GOD'S PROMISES:
Jeremiah 29:13		
Luke 10:27		

Loving the Lord with all your heart, soul, mind and strength—that's the first and only thing that really matters. Put first things first, and you will get the second things thrown in.

> *Lord God, You deserve first place. Fill me with an unquenchable thirst to know You and show me more of Yourself. I need You and love You. Amen.*

WEEK EIGHT: WHEN LIFE IS HARD

SCRIPTURE MEMORY VERSE

I have told you these things, so that in me you may have peace. In this world you will have trouble. But take heart! I have overcome the world.

John 16:33

Author Ronald Rohlheiser notes that crises of every kind "enter our lives not just as challenges to us to retain our balance and stability, but as invitations to stretch our hearts and minds."[1] These invitations, he says, can move us from being good people to becoming great people.

I've received several such invitations. The most significant found me in a Nepalese hospital on March 19, 1985. I had just undergone a C-section to deliver my second child, a daughter weighing barely five pounds. Stephanie was born with hydrocephalus—too much water on the brain. A surgeon said she needed a shunt in her head to drain the fluid, but he couldn't do the procedure there. The surgeon also suspected that she had heart issues, but he lacked the necessary equipment to run tests.

"You must return to North America on the first available flight," he said. That flight left in three days. The international airline considered me a "medical high-risk" and refused to issue me a ticket, so my husband bought a ticket for himself, wrapped our infant in a big blanket, packed a diaper bag and one bottle of breast milk, and headed home. I remained in Kathmandu with our twenty-month-old son for another week.

Saying goodbye to my newborn, not knowing whether she would survive, was the most difficult thing I have ever done. Add to that the uncertainty of an unknown future—Gene had no job, and we had neither home nor car. Our child would be admitted to the NICU ward of an American hospital, and we had no health insurance. Utter helplessness threatened to envelop me. Tears rolled as I prayed, "Father, what is happening? What do You want me to learn?"

There are basically two mindsets we can adopt in regard to adversity. If we adopt a "closed mindset," we will yearn for personal affirmation and be threatened and discouraged by obstacles and hardships. We will fear our adversity will expose character weaknesses, inability to cope, and, ultimately, our failure. However, if we adopt an "open mindset," we will view adversity as opportunity for growth and personal development and not become easily discouraged. There will be no such thing as failure for us but only learning opportunities.[2]

I knew nothing about this research back then. I only knew I had to choose to respond well or the enormity of our situation would wreck me. Have you ever felt like that?

This week's memory verse says we will have trouble in the world. Crises of every kind will find us sooner or later. Our mindset will determine our response to those crises. Our response will affect others around us and shape who we become and the legacy we leave. So, let's look at hardships through a biblical perspective. What does God think about them? How do our thoughts compare with His? What difference does it make?

— DAY 1: IS PEACE WITH FOOD POSSIBLE?

Lord, adversity and peace seem like polar opposites. How is it possible to experience peace of mind and soul when life turns upside down? Amen.

I've encountered folks who believe that following Christ means their problems will disappear. Their finances will never lack, their health will never wane, and their relationships will never disappoint. This would perhaps be true in a perfect world, but not in ours. The Bible never promises Christians an easy life. It does, however, guarantee peace even in the midst of pain. Write this memory verse for this week. Underline the words "you may have peace." Circle the words that say where you will find it.

_____

_____

_____

_____

Compare this with John 14:27. From where does this supernatural peace come?

___

___

___

The world pursues peace in a variety of different ways. For example, North Americans spend billions each year on health-related products, thinking peace will come if they feel and look better. But the peace to which Jesus referred isn't gained through a product. It is independent of circumstances. He modeled this truth and spoke promises of peace, knowing He would face crucifixion in a few hours.

We might say, "Well, Jesus was God, and knew how the story would end. That's why He could talk about peace at a time like that." Think again. Jesus faced a torturous death beyond the scope of our imagination. Read Luke 22:41–44. How would you describe His trauma?

___

___

___

Reread John 14:27. Jesus didn't promise to create peace for His disciples. He said He would share the peace that was His. Imagine the depth of this peace—and it's yours if you want it! For what situation in your life right now would you like Christ's peace?

___

___

___

___

Some of us feel desperate when it comes to having peace with food. We're tired of spending energy thinking about it. We're weary of trying to resist the temptation it poses. We're frustrated with its control over us. Is peace possible in this context?

The answer is yes. We begin to receive this peace when we admit our need for Christ's help. This peace grows as we allow Him to control and change our thoughts and desires. It increases as we reap the rewards for giving Him first place rather than food. Friendship with Jesus brings peace.

Read Isaiah 9:6. Jesus doesn't just possess peace. He is the _____ of _____ . The Hebrew word for peace is *shalom*, which infers complete inner calm that comes from harmony with God. What role does the Prince of Peace play in your having peace with God?

_____

_____

_____

_____

Back to John 14:27. Jesus commanded, "_____

_____ ." Jesus promises to give you peace, but you have a role. Now read Isaiah 26:3. In the *New Living Translation*, this verse reads, "You will keep in perfect peace all who trust in you, whose thoughts are fixed on you." What does it mean to keep your mind fixed on God?

_____

_____

_____

_____

Read Philippians 4:7 to find two other practical actions. Recall the equation you learned several weeks ago:_____ + _____ = _____ . How would you describe the depth of God's peace? Compare with the peace Jesus displayed hours before His crucifixion.

_____

_____

_____

_____

Has Christ been your go-to for peace? Or have you tried to find it in another source? Explain.

_____

_____

_____

_____

Father, be my Prince of Peace today and always. You alone. Amen.

— DAY 2: DID I DO SOMETHING WRONG?

Dear God, sometimes my problems feel like punishments. Give me Your perspective so I can learn from them and not carry unnecessary guilt or shame. Amen.

Two weeks after I returned from Nepal, I overheard my mother-in-law speaking with my mom. "I hope Grace doesn't think Stephanie's hydrocephalus is her fault," she said.

I had been meditating on Psalm 139:13–14 since Stephanie's birth, finding comfort and hope in the truth that God weaves our bodies together and His workmanship is marvelous. I believe the Holy Spirit—in His kindness—impressed those verses on me to align my thoughts with His thoughts from the outset. This was a gift, for I truly carried no self-blame. I wish I could say the same for other experiences.

Satan is a deceiver. He will contort anything to mess with your mind so you think contrary to God's truth. Here's a biblical example. Read John 9:1–3. Who was walking with Jesus when they saw the blind man? What was their assumption (see verse 2)?

_____

_____

_____

_____

Compare the disciples' thoughts with those of the religious leaders in verse 34. The disciples had heard Jesus teach and seen Him heal the lame, feed thousands, and walk on water. You would think their spiritual perception would have been beyond exemplary, but it needed realignment.

How easily we form beliefs that miss the mark. Sometimes those beliefs are about others in crisis. For example, a friend of mine was diagnosed with lung cancer in her thirties. She told me that several people, upon learning of her diagnosis, assumed she had been a heavy smoker. In reality, she had never even held a cigarette. What misperceptions or judgments have you made about others' difficult circumstances, whether health-related or otherwise?

_____

_____

_____

_____

Perhaps others have wrongly judged you during a difficult time. If so, you're in good company. Read Isaiah 53:1–6. How do many people view Jesus' suffering and death (see verse 3)? What was the truth about His death (see verses 4–6)?

_____

_____

_____

Sometimes your mistaken beliefs may concern your own personal hardships. Think about a situation when you assumed false blame or guilt for something that was beyond your control. How did this affect you mentally, emotionally, spiritually, and even physically?

_____

_____

_____

Return to John 9:3. What reason did Jesus give for the man's blindness?

_____

_____

_____

Compare with Isaiah 53:10–11. What did God accomplish through His Son's anguish?

_____

_____

_____

In the *New Living Translation*, verse 11 reads, "When he sees all that is accomplished by his anguish, he will be satisfied." Wow! Having such a Christ-like perspective about adversities is the ultimate goal, but you face a problem in achieving it. Read Isaiah 55:8–9. What is that problem?

_____

_____

_____

_____

How might your thoughts about a current difficulty benefit from a realignment?

_____

_____

_____

_____

How has God done something extraordinary through a difficulty in your life?

_____

_____

_____

_____

> *Lord, You are wise beyond words. Your purposes are infinite and Your ways beyond understanding. Help me view hardship not as punishment but as an opportunity for You to do something extraordinary. Amen.*

— DAY 3: DON'T JUST GRIN AND BEAR IT

Dear Father, I'm never glad when adversity shows up. Please show me things for which I can be thankful when it arrives. Amen.

Stephanie underwent eleven surgeries in her first two years. Spending that much time at her hospital bedside meant I had to find care for our son Matthew. By now we had no family nearby, so we depended on our neighbors' availability. Sometimes that worked well, but sometimes it didn't.

My husband would come to visit Stephanie after his workday ended. We would kiss hello and goodbye, and then I would drive thirty miles home to care for Matt. Gene returned home near midnight, and we would collapse in bed. The next morning, we would get up and repeat the same process. In the midst of this, Stephanie's neurosurgeon and occupational therapist died suddenly in separate incidents. Life was hard.

No doubt you have a hardship story too. Maybe cancer? Divorce? Bankruptcy? The loss of a loved one? Adversity strikes, and you might think it's an evil meant to be endured. You want to wish it away. But is this how God wants you to view challenges? Read James 1:2–4. How are you to consider trials of every kind?

_____

_____

_____

In the *New Living Translation,* this verse reads, "Whenever trouble comes your way, let it be an opportunity for joy." What are five reasons you can be joyful in the midst of a hardship?

_____

_____

_____

One reason we can have joy is that our trials develop perseverance, or endurance as stated in the *New Living Translation*. The Greek word translated *perseverance* implies steadfastness, to be unflinching, or to hold one's ground. When used in the military sense, it implies soldiers defending their territory. The enemy pounds and pummels, but the soldiers stand their ground indefinitely until the enemy retreats.

As Rick Renner writes, "The Early Church called patience [perseverance] the 'queen of all virtues.'"[3] The believers knew if they possessed this quality, it wasn't a question of if they would win their battles but when they would win. According to James 1:4, what happens as you cooperate with God when He allows hardships in your life?

_____

_____

_____

Read Romans 5:3–4. What does it mean to glory in your sufferings (see verse 3)?

_____

_____

_____

According to this passage, suffering produces _____ , perseverance produces _____ , and character produces _____ . On what is your hope based?

_____

_____

_____

_____

Read 1 Thessalonians 5:18. What is another attitude you are to demonstrate in hardships?

I never gave thanks for my baby's medical needs. Instead, I thanked God for His presence, provision, and promise to be faithful no matter what. For what can you be thankful in a hardship you face?

Read Ephesians 5:18–20. How has God enabled you to view trials with thankfulness?

What actions can you take to ensure your thoughts and attitudes are God-honoring when you are facing adversity?

_____

_____

_____

_____

_____

Lord, fill me with Your Spirit so I can view hardships with joy and gratitude. Amen.

— DAY 4: DOES GOD CARE?

Dear Father, sometimes I question Your intent toward me. Change my thinking from doubt to belief. Amen.

Our pediatrician was away when ten-month-old Stephanie suddenly grew feverish and lethargic. His associate misdiagnosed her on two consecutive visits to the clinic. I took Stephanie a third time within forty-eight hours of the first visit. By then our pediatrician had returned, and he did a spinal tap. Sure enough, she had meningitis. Thus began a month-long hospital stay with two surgeries.

A week after her release, Stephanie was to undergo a previously scheduled brain surgery. Two days before the operation, her neurosurgeon was killed in a helicopter skiing accident. An associate we had never met stepped in to perform the six-hour procedure.

For six weeks after the operation, Stephanie wore arm splints so she couldn't bump her head with her hands. I had to tie her outstretched arms to the crib siderails at naptime and nighttime. Doing so left me feeling like an abusive mother.

At times I questioned God's goodness. Where was He? Did He even care about our daughter? But the Holy Spirit refocused my thoughts by reminding me of the truths found in Scripture. Read Psalm 29:10–11. Who is king over the floodwaters? How would you apply this to adversity?

What does God give His people? With what does He bless them?

How have you experienced God's strength and peace in hardship?

Read Psalm 33:18–22. To whom does this promise apply (see verse 18)? What actions does the Lord take on their behalf?

In the *New Living Translation*, verse 22 reads, "Let your unfailing love surround us, Lord." What visual image do these words bring to mind? What gives you the ability to rejoice?

_____

_____

_____

_____

Read Psalm 34:17–19. Whose cries for help does the Lord hear? What actions does He take on their behalf?

_____

_____

_____

_____

_____

Read Psalm 56:8–9. How can you know God is near and aware of your pain (see verse 8)? How can your thoughts become your enemy (see verse 9)?

_____

_____

_____

_____

_____

"God is for me." Speak this phrase aloud and with confidence. How does it instill confidence in God's care for you?

_____

_____

_____

Read 2 Corinthians 1:3–5. Look up the words *compassion* and *comfort* in a thesaurus. Now write three synonyms for each:

God is the Father of compassion: _____ _____ _____

God is the Father of comfort: _____ _____ _____

Which of these synonyms resonates with you? Why?

_____

_____

_____

_____

Look up the word *abound* in a dictionary. What does this say about the measure of God's care for you when you are experiencing hardship? What are you to do with the overflow of divine comfort? What does this say about God's care for others too?

_____

_____

_____

Doubting God's care will leave you feeling alone, burdened, afraid, or perhaps angry about your situation. How easy it is to fall into negative thoughts and behaviors, especially those related to food. Faulty thinking will say you deserve to satisfy your cravings because the emotional burden you carry is so heavy. But living from the truth will change your perspective. It will help keep your focus on God's power to strengthen and deliver you rather than expecting food to do that for you. Make Romans 8:35–37 personal by reading it aloud. What is the truth about God's goodness in the context of adversities?

_____

_____

_____

God, thank You for being my ever-present help in time of need. Thank You for caring. Amen.

— DAY 5: WILL IT EVER END?

Precious Father, it's difficult to keep the right perspective when it feels as though the pain will never end. I need hope. Amen.

Hospitalizations, medical appointments, and therapy sessions filled our calendar after Stephanie's birth. Every time she spiked a fever, I questioned whether her shunt had become infected. If she vomited, I wondered if her shunt had blocked and she would need another surgery. She had little muscle tone in her legs, so she didn't walk until she was two years old. Those things, combined with other challenges, sometimes made me think the stress would never ease. On those days, I had to take my what-if negative thoughts captive and replace them with the truth to fight the despair.

Read 1 Peter 1:6–7. Peter wrote this letter to encourage believers experiencing severe persecution for their faith. His words reminded them that their hope was

MYplace O BIBLE STUDY

in Jesus and God would honor them for trusting Him in their suffering. What did Peter say would help them find purpose for their pain? What would be the outcome if they remained strong?

_____

_____

_____

How long did Peter say their trials would last?

_____

_____

_____

Read 1 Peter 5:10. Again, how long did Peter say the believers' suffering would last? What did he say God would do after this period of time had passed?

_____

_____

_____

Read 2 Corinthians 4:17–18. Paul said our troubles are _____ and _____ . Yet when we're in the midst of them, our thoughts will tell us otherwise. What do they say?

_____

_____

_____

How can you stand against wrong thinking (see verse 18)?

_____

_____

_____

Someday, you will experience joys that will make today's pain seem totally insignificant. What might those joys be?

_____

_____

_____

When it comes to your physical well-being, the disciplines required to regain your health might feel burdensome or painful, but don't give up or lose hope. Persevere and you will experience the joys that personal transformation brings. What are three joys you anticipate? (One example from my experience is the simple joy of walking uphill without feeling out of breath.)

_____

_____

_____

Read Hebrews 12:1–3 and compare with 2 Corinthians 4:17–18. What joy did Jesus anticipate that made Him willing to die on the cross?

_____

_____

_____

Jesus knew His death would result in eternal life for all who trust Him for salvation. How would your attitude toward suffering change if you knew it would result in someone's salvation?

___

___

___

___

You are to throw off any weight that hinders you from running the race. What misperceptions about adversity might be limiting what God wants to do in your life through those trials?

___

___

___

___

Sometimes it's hard to know what to pray when you are treading the waters of adversity. If that has been your experience, let me encourage you to pray this promise: "Father, I don't know when this situation will end. Protect me, shield me, and fortify my heart and my mind from the what-ifs and negative anticipation. Thank You in advance that in Your perfect timing, You will restore, support, and strengthen me in every way. Put my feet on a firm foundation for Your glory. Amen."

> *God, use my pain for someone's eternal gain. Please make it all worthwhile. Amen.*

— DAY 6: REFLECTION AND APPLICATION

Dear Lord, I wish You would let me see what You're doing in the spiritual realm so I could understand why You allow painful situations in my life. Amen.

Sometimes we suffer for doing wrong. Making bad choices means we pay consequences. We reap what we sow. However, as we discussed in Day 2, sometimes we suffer for doing what is right. That is when we tend to question God's wisdom. Does He care about us and what's happening? Is He really a good, good, father like the song lyrics say? Is He truly trustworthy, or does He need our help in this matter?

Next to Jesus, Job is a supreme example of suffering for doing what is right. Read Job 1:1, 4–5 and 29:7–25. How would you summarize his character?

_____

_____

_____

_____

Read Job 1:8. How did God view Job?

_____

_____

_____

_____

Why did God allow such extreme adversity if He loved and respected Job (see verses 8–12)?

What losses did Job suffer (see 1:13–19; 2:4–8)? How did Job respond (see 1:20–22; 2:10)?

Job and his friends engaged in theological debate about the goings-on until God stepped in and challenged Job with a litany of questions (see 38:1–41:34). That was when Job realized how little he understood of God's wisdom and ways, and he repented of behaving as though he knew more than he did (see 42:1–5).

The story includes nothing about God offering Job an explanation for the pain he had experienced. Instead, God asked Job questions he couldn't answer. By doing so, it's as if God was saying, "I'm wiser and bigger and stronger than you, so please trust Me even when you don't understand." When was time you suffered for doing what was right? How did you respond?

What did you learn about God's character through the experience?

_____

_____

_____

_____

In what ways has God shown you why He allowed your pain?

_____

_____

_____

_____

How has God used your experience in an unexpected way?

_____

_____

_____

God doesn't owe us an explanation for allowing adversity. He has never revealed His purpose for my daughter being born with multiple medical issues. (By the way, Stephanie is married and doing well, though she still has the shunt.) Perhaps someday, in heaven, God will tell us why He allowed pain in our lives. That would be nice, but I suspect worshiping in His presence will wipe away our need to know.

> *Lord Jesus, I choose to trust You even when I can't understand why You allow adversity. I cling to You, the all-wise God. Amen.*

— DAY 7: REFLECTION AND APPLICATION

Dear Lord, at times I feel as though life has treated me unfairly. It seems others have no major problems, and I wish I could change places with them. Amen.

Stephanie was five months old when we visited my sister-in-law one afternoon. She was eight months pregnant and eagerly anticipating the baby's arrival.

I listened as she talked about preparing the baby's room. A little voice in my head whispered, "It's not fair. She has it all—a new home, a good-paying job, a cute little sports car. And she'll have a healthy baby too. Being a missionary wasn't worth it, was it? You have none of those things, and you spend half your life sitting in clinics and hospitals. Poor you!"

It took only a few seconds to recognize who whispered those words, and I had only a few seconds to choose my response. Letting them linger would lead me down a path to becoming a jealous, bitter wife and mother. I had to reject them and replace them with God's words—words of truth.

Satan pulled a similar ploy on Asaph. Pause for a minute to read Psalm 73. You'll see how it describes the tussle in his thinking as he watched evil people prosper. "Here I am, trying to live a pure life, and God rewards me with pain. Other people do whatever they please in direct opposition to God's truth, and they enjoy health and wealth. It's not fair, God!"

Trying to understand the discrepancy left Asaph troubled and confused. When and how did his thoughts clear (see verse 17)?

_____

_____

_____

_____

_____

Time in God's presence changed Asaph's mind. How did he describe his thoughts prior to aligning them with truth (see verses 21–22)?

_____

_____

_____

Asaph turned from envy, grief, and bitterness to worship. Read verses 23–26. What are at least three truths in which he found encouragement?

_____

_____

_____

It is easy to fall into thinking that life has dealt you an unfair deck. You compare your situation to others' circumstances and lose proper perspective. There's only one thing that can guard you against Satan's subtle mental attacks. What is it?

_____

_____

_____

Can you relate to the struggle Asaph (and I) had with comparing our troubles with other people's situations? If so, what thoughts have gone through your mind?

_____

_____

_____

Relate this to your First Place for Health journey. How have you compared your progress to those whose progress seems easier or faster? How have you responded to those thoughts?

_____

_____

_____

If you've rejected those thoughts and replaced them with God's truth, that's great! If not, then reread Psalm 73:23–26 and choose one truth that especially resonates with you. Write it on a sticky note and post it where you will see it often. Ask the Holy Spirit to bring it to your mind every time the enemy feeds you a lie.

> *God, my mind is prone to comparison. Guard me from wishing I could walk another person's journey, and help me to fully appreciate the one You've chosen for me. Amen.*

WEEK EIGHT WHEN LIFE IS HARD

WEEK NINE: IT'S NOT ALL ABOUT ME

SCRIPTURE MEMORY VERSE
Do nothing out of selfish ambition or vain conceit. Rather, in humility value others above yourselves, not looking to your own interests but each of you to the interests of the others.
                                                            Philippians 2:3–4

My youngest daughter, Kim, was about eight years old when she said, "Mom, what would it be like if our thoughts about other people flashed above our heads in neon lights?"

Eek! I recalled my thoughts about the woman sitting in front of me at church the Sunday before. It looks like she chose her outfit with her eyes closed. *Hey, she's a perfect candidate for a total makeover contest!*

I remembered the chatty clerk at the grocery store. *I don't need to hear your entire life story. Just bag the food, please. I have places to go and things to do.*

I recalled my last appointment at the hair salon. I watched the stylist—the gal who had done my hair every six weeks for three years—part my hair on the opposite side to where I always part it. *She does this every time. Why can't she get it right?*

My child's innocence revealed my lack thereof. It also revealed wisdom that's worth considering as we talk about our thoughts and our need to align them with God's thoughts within the context of our relationships.

Here's another piece of wisdom, spoken by Frederick W. Faber, the noted English theologian and hymn writer who penned "Faith of Our Fathers." He said, "Kind thoughts are rarer than either kind words or deeds. They imply a great deal of thinking about others. This in itself is rare. But they also imply a great deal of thinking about others without the thoughts being criticisms. This is rarer still."[1]

The memory verse for this week tells us to value others above ourselves. Doing so begins in our mind, by thinking kind thoughts about the people God has placed in our lives. When our thoughts are wholesome and selfless, our actions and motives bring a smile to God's face.

Psalm 139:17 states, "How precious are your thoughts about me, O God! They are innumerable!" (NLT). If God's thoughts about us are precious and we are to be His imitators, then guess what? Our thoughts toward His children should be precious as well. That leaves no room for critical thoughts, jealousy, envy, lust, greed—you name it. He values us, and we are to therefore value others. And it all begins in our minds.

This week, we will expose faulty thinking in the context of relationships, and we will fill our minds with truth that transforms. After all, I know that if my thoughts about others were to flash in neon lights, I would want them to be pure and inspirational. How about you?

— DAY 1: LOOKS AREN'T EVERYTHING

Dear God, I'm prone to judge others based on their appearance. Teach me to think about them as You do. Amen.

My daughter and I were walking in our city park when we noticed several rough-looking guys clustered under a tree. They wore T-shirts and black leather vests. Some wore bandanas on their heads. My first thought was, *Obviously they are part of a motorcycle gang.*

The sidewalk led us within a few feet of the group. That's when I saw the emblem on the back of their vests. These guys weren't gangsters! They were members of a Christian motorcycle association.

How quickly our thoughts jump to wrong conclusions about others based on their facial features, clothing, size, or posture. When was an instance when you judged someone wrongly based on their looks?

_____

_____

_____

_____

_____

Read 1 Samuel 16:1–13. Samuel misjudged when he searched for a king for Israel. He took one look at Jesse's eldest son and assumed that he was God's anointed. What physical characteristics might have led him to think this about Eliab?

_____

_____

_____

_____

What did the Lord say Samuel was not to consider (see verse 7)?

_____

_____

_____

_____

Complete the last sentence of verse 7: "People look at the _____, but the LORD looks at the _____." Now read 1 Samuel 17:8–1. Eliab was a soldier in the Israelite army. What did difficult circumstances reveal about his heart condition (see verse 11)?

_____

_____

_____

_____

_____

Compare with verse 28. How would you describe Eliab's heart as evidenced by his attitude and words toward David? What might have been the outcome if Samuel had anointed Eliab as king?

_____

_____

_____

_____

It's tempting to assume that people who are physically attractive have everything together. In reality, they might be struggling with the same issues with which many of us wrestle—shame, lust, pride, fear, perfectionism, food addictions, and more. On the flip side, we might look at people considered ordinary or unattractive by society's standards and assume they are incapable, less intelligent, or even less valuable than others when, in fact, nothing could be further from the truth. Read 1 Samuel 17:32-47. How did Saul view David (see verse 33)? How did Goliath view David (see verses 41-42)?

_____

_____

_____

_____

How would you describe David's heart? How did he differ from the onlookers' perspectives (see verses 34-40, 45-47)?

_____

_____

_____

Saul and Goliath's focus on David's appearance caused them to underestimate him and God's power working through his life. How might you do the same thing to others?

_____

_____

_____

Read 1 Corinthians 1:27–29 and fill in the blanks:

God chooses the _____. Man prefers the _____.

God chooses the _____. Man prefers the _____.

God chooses the _____, the _____,

and the things that _____. Man prefers the _____.

Why do you think God often chooses to use people whom others overlook (see verse 29)?

_____

_____

_____

Let's be cautious to not form wrong conclusions about people based on what we see. Instead, let's ask God to give us His eyes when we look at others.

> *Lord, guard my heart from misjudging people. Give me Your eyes and Your heart so I might see them as You do. Amen.*

— DAY 2: WASHING JUDAS'S FEET

Jesus, You set the standard high for treating others well. Fill and control my thoughts, for only then will I treat others as You did when You walked this earth. Amen.

It's easy to treat others well when we feel they deserve it. The challenge comes when they hurt us or someone we love. Our minds tell us to strike back in self-defense. We hold imaginary conversations with the offender, during which we speak the words we wish we had said in real life. Our minds might insist we cut that difficult person out of our lives.

Some testy relationships need strict boundaries, but many improve with godly wisdom and patience. Our goal is to have healthy relationships, because God created us to thrive in community. We need people to build into our lives, and they need us to do the same.

But how are we to regard that person who is hard to love—the one who seems bent on making our lives challenging? Read John 13:1–17. What is the main focus of this story?

___

___

___

The men had walked dusty streets littered with garbage and animal waste. Imagine the smell as they gathered around the table for supper. And imagine their shock when Jesus stooped to wash their feet—a task usually relegated to the lowest servant. Jesus' actions were remarkable considering His true identity. But another factor made them even more amazing. What was that (see John 13:10–11 and compare with Luke 22:21–22)?

___

___

Jesus told the group that a betrayer was sitting in their midst. What is the significance of the disciples' response (see Luke 22:23)?

_____

_____

Jesus knew Judas would betray Him, but He treated him no differently than the others. You might think this came easy for Him, because He was God. Read Hebrews 4:15. How do you think Jesus might have actually felt?

_____

_____

Loving someone who has hurt you will require more strength and integrity than you can muster. Read John 13:1–3. What enabled Jesus to show love to Judas?

_____

_____

Jesus was grounded and secure in His relationship with the Father. He had nothing to prove except that love conquers all, which freed Him to serve Judas. Compare this to your life. How does being secure in your spiritual identity influence your relationships—especially with challenging people?

_____

_____

Understanding your spiritual identity will contribute to your emotional well-being and ultimately your ability to enjoy healthy interpersonal relationships. Take this thought a step further. How does it contribute to your physical health?

_____

_____

_____

Read John 13:13–17. Jesus' actions show that He had said, "I love you," in His mind. How are you to emulate His attitude with hard-to-love people? What is the promised outcome (see verse 17)?

_____

_____

_____

Ask God how you can demonstrate love to the "Judas" in your life. Write down what He says.

_____

_____

_____

_____

> *Lord, cleanse me from negative thoughts about people who have hurt me in the past. Make me more like Jesus and fill me with Your love for them. Amen.*

— DAY 3: HONORING GOD; HONORING OTHERS

Dear Lord, thank You for giving instructions about engaging with people. Teach me how to live beyond myself in a self-centered world. Amen.

I once interviewed Dr. Gary Smalley to glean his insights on relationships. He said something I'll always remember: "A healthy relationship cannot exist without honor. Imagine a scale that measures a person's level of importance from one to ten. If we consider ourselves an eight on the scale, then we must consider others a nine. To honor others means we consider them more important than ourselves."

This principle teaches a concept contrary to our human nature. Our minds tell us to look out for number one. Satisfy our needs. Ensure our comfort. Guarantee our happiness. But God's Word says otherwise. Read Romans 12:10. Use a thesaurus to find several synonyms for the verb form of honor, and list them below.

_____

_____

_____

Read the following verses and fill in the chart.

VERSE:	TO WHOM ARE WE TO SHOW HONOR?	TRUTH ABOUT GOD:
Leviticus 19:32		
Romans 13:1		
Ephesians 6:2-3		

WEEK NINE IT'S NOT ALL ABOUT ME

VERSE:	TO WHOM ARE WE TO SHOW HONOR?	TRUTH ABOUT GOD:
Ephesians 6:5-9		
1 Timothy 5:17-18		
Hebrews 13:4		

We are commanded to show honor, but sometimes the one whom we are to honor doesn't seem worthy. Our human way of thinking then adopts and justifies dishonoring attitudes and behaviors. Read 1 Samuel 24:1-10. David's men encouraged him to seize the opportunity to topple King Saul. After all, they reasoned, God had appointed David as the next king of Israel. This was his chance to secure his rightful position. How did David respond (see verse 4)?

_____

_____

_____

_____

What did he feel moments later (see verses 5-6)? How did his desire to honor the Lord influence his behavior toward King Saul (see verses 8-9)?

_____

_____

_____

_____

What freed David to honor Saul even though the king didn't deserve it (see verses 12, and 15)?

David honored the Lord. He was therefore able to respect Saul as God's anointed until the Lord removed him from the throne. Make this personal. How might your thoughts about who God is help you respect someone who doesn't seem worthy?

Read Revelation 4:11. Why does God deserve your honor?

Read Romans 1:21–25. What are several things that happen when you fail to honor your Creator as He deserves?

Failing to honor God will make you vulnerable to Satan's lies and the consequences of believing them. On the flipside, read 1 Samuel 2:30. What is the reward for honoring God?

_____

_____

_____

Read Isaiah 29:13. To what degree does God want you to honor Him?

_____

_____

_____

Now read 1 Corinthian 6:19-20 and apply this to your wellness journey. God is your Creator, and He has given you only one body. What is one action you can take this week to honor Him by caring for your body? How can you can honor the members of your First Place for Health group as they pursue their wellness goals?

> *Father, You are worthy of all my honor and praise. Teach me to honor You with everything that I am, and then fulfill Your promise to honor my obedience. Amen.*

— DAY 4: HONESTY

Lord, create in me a willingness to be vulnerable about my struggles even though it is humbling to do so. Amen.

C.S. Lewis said, "Friendship . . . is born at that moment when one person says to another: 'What! You too? I thought I was the only one.'"[2]

Honesty in our relationships brings empowerment. Telling others about our struggles gives them permission to be transparent with us as well. This invites mutual encouragement through prayer, support, and accountability. There is strength in knowing someone's got our back and loves us despite our flaws. Sounds like a First Place for Health group, right?

However, speaking from experience, our human bent resists honesty. It succumbs to the fear of rejection, and we respond by wearing a façade. We believe the lie that says people will think less of us if they know our imperfections. We become experts at wearing masks with plastic smiles to cover our pain. But how does this mindset compare with the truth? Read Proverbs 16:18. In what is the fear of rejection rooted? What is the outcome of pride?

_____

_____

_____

_____

Now read 1 Peter 5:5–10. What is God's response to the proud? How does He respond to the humble (see verses 5–6)?

_____

_____

_____

What does humility look like within the context of your First Place for Health group?

_____

_____

_____

Based on verse 8, and within the context of today's discussion, what are three lies the devil might use to destroy you?

_____

_____

_____

In verse 9, Peter says you are to take a firm stand against the devil and be strong in your faith. What is one practical action you can take in obedience to these commands?

_____

_____

_____

How does knowing that fellow Christians are experiencing the same struggles encourage you?

_____

_____

_____

What is the promise found in verse 10? To whom did God make this promise—the proud or the humble? Explain.

_____

_____

_____

_____

It isn't easy to be vulnerable and honest about your struggles. You may worry about how others will respond when they hear your story. Will they accept you, or will they judge and reject you? These are justifiable concerns, because human nature is to shame, criticize, cast blame, or develop opinions based on inaccurate understanding. Read Romans 15:5–7. How do you need to shift your thinking to ensure others feel safe with transparency?

_____

_____

_____

_____

Who helps you respond as you should? Who does the outcome glorify?

_____

_____

_____

_____

Compare Romans 15:5–7 with Romans 12:9–10. What does loving others with genuine affection look like when they open their hearts to you?

_____

_____

_____

Sometimes honesty takes a different angle. Read Galatians 6:1–3. What might hinder you from being honest with someone you know is stuck in destructive behaviors? What should your attitude and approach be when you reach out to help?

_____

_____

_____

_____

How do Paul's words in Romans 12:9–10 apply to a situation such as this?

_____

_____

_____

_____

> *Father God, thank You that I never need fear being honest with You. Help others feel the same way about me. Amen.*

DAY 5: BE A PEACEMAKER

Father God, it must hurt You to see Your children bicker. Make me a peacemaker so I can promote healing in Your family. Amen.

Joni Eareckson Tada says, "Believers are never told to become one; we already are one and are expected to act like it."[3]

Now, that's an example of a godly mindset. Unfortunately, not all God's family members think this way. In the wake of pursuing personal interests, we ignore our Father's wisdom and instruction about how to get along. The result is misunderstandings, relationship fall-outs, and unnecessary pain. This is not how God wants His family to function.

In Romans 12:18, Paul writes, "If it is possible, as far as it depends on you, live at peace with everyone." Circle the phrase that reflects God's heart for relationships, and then underline the two phrases that imply this is a challenge. Now read Romans 16:20, 1 Thessalonians 5:23, and Hebrews 13:20. How is God described in these verses?

_____

_____

_____

_____

Compare these with Colossians 1:20. Why does God value peace?

_____

_____

_____

_____

God is a God of peace by nature. When you enter into a relationship with Him, He comes to live in you through His Holy Spirit. Read Galatians 5:22–23. What are the character qualities He produces in you when you give Him the freedom to do so? Circle the third quality listed.

_____

_____

_____

_____

In the physical realm, children bear a resemblance to their parents. In the spiritual realm, God's children also bear their Father's resemblance. This grows more pronounced as we mature in our faith. Read Romans 12:2. How does this happen?

_____

_____

_____

_____

God transforms you by changing your mind, cleansing and renewing it with His truth. He takes your old life filled with self-centered thoughts and wrong beliefs and replaces it with the new. You begin to value what He values—peace in relationships. And you begin to model His peace-making nature. Read Matthew 5:9. What title does God bestow on those who work for peace?

_____

_____

_____

_____

This means that God's children value peace and demonstrate this quality. What does a lack of this quality and pursuit in a believer's life indicate? What is the remedy?

_____

_____

_____

_____

God wants us to pursue peace in our relationships because peace reflects His nature. When we're at odds with someone, we would rather not talk with them or look them in the eye, but God expects more from us. He expects us to build relationship bridges. But here's a caution: not at all costs. Read James 3:17–18. What are the characteristics of godly wisdom?

_____

_____

_____

_____

What characteristic precedes "peace loving?" Compare with Matthew 5:8–9.

_____

_____

_____

_____

Your peace-making efforts should never compromise God's truth. Obedience to Him always comes first. How might you be tempted to sacrifice purity for peace in a difficult relationship?

_____

_____

_____

Peace-making doesn't always achieve peace. What are some ways to continue to reflect God's nature even when your efforts don't succeed?

_____

_____

_____

> *Father, please give me godly wisdom and unconditional love as I seek to build, not burn, relationship bridges. Amen.*

— DAY 6: REFLECTION AND APPLICATION

Dear Lord, thank You for giving instructions about how to have healthy interpersonal relationships. Please help me to see others through Your eyes and empower me to treat them as You say I should. Amen.

On Day 3, we talked about honoring others above ourselves. Let's delve a little deeper into that topic by looking at different translations of Romans 12:10. Comparing a Bible text in several versions is like examining a diamond from different angles. All combined, they show us the gem's true beauty. Here goes . . .

> Be devoted to one another in love.
> Honor one another above yourselves (NIV).
>
> Be good friends who love deeply; practice playing second fiddle (MSG).
>
> Love one another with brotherly affection; outdo one another in showing honor (RSV).
>
> Love each other with genuine affection, and take delight in honoring each other (NLT).

Putting several versions together like this helps paint a more complete picture of what Paul is teaching here—especially about the attitude with which we're to love others. Doing it with rolled eyes—"Okay, okay, I'll do it if I have to"—or gritted teeth—"Sheesh, loving her is almost more than I can bear"—isn't exactly what God has in mind.

Honoring others God's way means intentionally looking for ways to esteem them. It means taking delight in blessing them, not considering it something we have to do to earn God's good favor. It means going the extra mile and putting forth our best effort to make them feel loved. Which one of these texts resonates most with you? Why?

_____

_____

_____

What is one way you can apply this text in a relationship with a member of your immediate or extended family, a co-worker, a neighbor, or a person who serves as part of his or her job?

_____

_____

_____

Write the text of your choice on a card and post it where you will see it often. Make it a daily prayer.

> Father, I welcome You to adjust my attitude. Remove selfish thoughts and replace them with thoughts of how to best honor other people. Grant me simple and creative ideas that will truly bless others. Amen.

— DAY 7: REFLECTION AND APPLICATION

Dear God, You embody love—pure, selfless, and unconditional. I want to bear Your resemblance, but I can't do it on my own. I need You to fill me and flow through me. Amen.

As I write this, I'm sitting in a friend's living room several hours' drive from my place. I'm scheduled to speak at a local women's retreat beginning tomorrow, but I had to come early for an appointment.

Arriving early meant finding somewhere to stay overnight. When I contacted my friend last week about the possibility of staying with her, she said, "My hubby and I are leaving on vacation, so we won't be in town. But that doesn't matter. We'll give you our security code, and you can make yourselves at home. Help yourself to whatever's in the fridge." Her hospitality warmed my heart and made me feel loved.

I did the same thing last summer for a young couple who work with our mission organization. They had packed up their four little kids and driven several thousand miles visiting family and ministry supporters. They had asked about visiting us, too, but their schedule meant arriving while we were out of town. A thought came to mind as we tried to make our schedule fit theirs: *Offer them your house. It doesn't matter if you're not there.*

The young wife heaved an audible sigh when we asked if they would be okay with staying there without us for a couple of days. "Absolutely," she said. "We're exhausted and could use some time alone as a family." My husband told them where to find the spare key, I stocked the fridge, and they felt loved—just like I feel tonight.

Loving others takes many forms. It means babysitting occasionally to provide a single mom with a much-needed break. It means volunteering to drive cancer patients to and from their chemo treatments and sitting with them if they want company.

Love means preparing meals for a shut-in, shoveling a neighbor's sidewalk, or greeting the grocery store clerk with a cheery hello. For my ten-year-old granddaughter, love means growing her hair long so she can donate it to a charity that designs wigs for kids with cancer.

Love means listening with undivided attention, refusing to engage in gossip, extending forgiveness even though the offender didn't ask for it, and getting up at night to calm a frightened child. Love means not feeling slighted when someone else takes credit that is rightfully ours, saying yes when the Holy Spirit prompts us to open conversation with a stranger, and getting our hands dirty performing a task no one else wants.

Love is not making others revolve around us. It is living the Golden Rule: "Treat others as you want to be treated." How do you want to be treated today? How can you live the Golden Rule in practical terms?

_____

_____

_____

Father God, teach me to live by the Golden Rule, to always be mindful of treating others as I wish to be treated. Amen.

WEEK NINE IT'S NOT ALL ABOUT ME

WEEK TEN: FORGIVENESS: WHAT IT IS, WHAT IT IS NOT

SCRIPTURE MEMORY VERSE

And forgive us our debts, as we also have forgiven our debtors.

Matthew 6:12

Every time I develop a new workshop or keynote presentation, something happens that forces me to process and internalize my words. That's good and necessary, but sometimes it's downright painful. This time, I had been asked to present a lecture on forgiveness. I wasn't surprised, then, when a woman with whom I'd had a complicated relationship for more than two decades phoned the evening before I had planned to prepare my materials.

She hurled one false accusation after another. Most of what she said seemed irrational. The call lasted two hours. I let it die a natural death, because ending it would have made matters worse. My mind followed its human bent and replayed the accusations she had made against me in the past. "I just want her to be sorry for saying those things," I said to my husband as I got ready for bed.

That conversation was the first thing on my mind when I woke from a not-so-sweet sleep the next morning. That's when I realized how I had allowed this person and her issues to control me. I faced a choice: let resentment simmer and boil until it spilled over and stained other relationships, or deal with my emotions appropriately. I knew the right approach meant working through forgiveness. I had to practice what I hoped to preach.

Forgiving people who hurt us is a non-negotiable. We do it as a matter of obedience to honor God who has forgiven us and commands us to do likewise. We also do it because anything less hinders us from becoming the people God created us to be. Allowing wounds to fester affects our mental, emotional, spiritual, and physical health. At the root of many food-related issues lies unresolved pain or anger. Rather than learning how to deal appropriately with our emotions, we choose to eat them instead.

God created us to flourish, and forgiveness plays a vital role in our ability to do so. Even more, God is forgiving in nature, and calling Him our Father means we are to bear His resemblance. We are to demonstrate the same characteristics He possesses. The ability to forgive—even when others don't deserve it—is one of those traits.

Forgiveness is not easy. It defies our way of thinking—that we're justified in feeling angry toward our offenders. We may even want to seek revenge. After all, they've inflicted a wound. They deserve a payback. They deserve to feel a bit of the pain they've caused. But God's truth says otherwise, and there begins the tussle between our perception of what is right and fair and what is truly right and fair.

The gal I mentioned earlier is still a part of my life. Our relationship is slowly improving. Aligning my thoughts with God's thoughts about forgiveness has played a role.

I pray this week's study will provide fresh and encouraging insights on forgiveness so you can better deal with any tough situations you might face now or in the future.

—— DAY 1: GOD'S FORGIVING NATURE

Dear Father, I confess a limited understanding of who You are. Help me to not presume on Your mercy and forgiveness, but at the same time, help me never to doubt it. Amen.

I recall a spiritual conversation with a young woman of a different faith. When I told her about God's love and gift of forgiveness, she said, "That's great—for you. You're lucky to have a God like that. Mine is different, and because I was born into this religion, my spiritual journey and destiny is what it is."

Sadly, this woman believed forgiveness was not possible for her. No matter how hard she strived to be a good person, she knew she would always fall short of her god's standard. Inner freedom, joy, peace, and hope were unattainable for her as well.

I've met believers whose perception about forgiveness resembles this woman's. They feel as if they are spiritual washouts because they keep messing up no matter how hard they try to please God. They figure their sins will accumulate until, at some point, they will cross an invisible line where God says, "You've gone too far. No more forgiveness for you!"

Oh, how contrary those thoughts are to the truth about God's nature. Read Psalm 103:8–18. What does this passage reveal to you about God's character in the context of our tendency to sin and our need for forgiveness?

___

Compare with 1 John 1:9. What does this verse tell you about God's character? What little word in this verse refutes the misperception that you will cross a line where your sins become too many for God to forgive? Write it in capital letters.

___

Read Matthew 12:31–32. What one sin will God never forgive? Why is this the case?

___

God cannot act in a way contrary to His nature. He is holy, so He cannot tolerate sin. He is just, so therefore He must punish sin. But He is also loving and good, so therefore He forgives those who confess their sin. Read Luke 15:11–32. Who does the father represent? Who does the younger son represent?

___

What was the son's assumption about his father's response to his return (see verses 18–19)? What was the father's actual response (see verses 20, 22–24)?

The father saw his son from a long distance away (see verse 20). What does this infer about his heart for his child?

Perhaps you feel as though your failed efforts to control your food cravings have left you undeserving of God's love. You might even be afraid to ask God for help yet again. If that's your situation, how does His response to the prodigal apply to you?

Write a prayer of confession and thanksgiving. Confess any thoughts or behaviors that fall short of God's standard. Thank Him for showing you who He is and for His love that surpasses human understanding.

_____

_____

_____

_____

Dear God, I praise You because You are my faithful Father always willing to forgive. Help me hold fast to this truth so long as I walk this earth. Amen.

— DAY 2: GOD'S SOVEREIGNTY OVER MY CIRCUMSTANCES

Dear God, it's easy to feel angry when people do bad things that change other people's lives. Help me to know how to forgive in a situation like that. Amen.

A family friend died last week after battling a brain tumor. Months before, he suspected something was wrong and sought medical help. His doctor blamed the symptoms on stress and sent him home to rest. But the symptoms worsened, and the doctor finally ordered tests. The results showed an orange-sized tumor. My friend underwent surgery and treatment, but ultimately, it came too late.

Tragedy happens every day. Lives flip upside down, turn inside out, and never look the same. It's easy to become angry with those who play a role in doing this to us or those we love. How does a widow forgive the doctor who disregarded her husband's health concerns? How does a parent forgive the drunk driver whose actions claimed her child's life? How does a wife forgive the husband who chose an alternative lifestyle over their marriage? The list goes on and on. Fill in the blank with your own specifics:

How can I forgive _____ for _____ ?

Read Genesis 37. How old was Joseph when this story opens (see verse 2)? What caused a rift between him and his half-brothers (see verses 2–4, 5–8, 9–11)?

_____

_____

_____

_____

What did his brother finally do (see verses 18–20, 23–28)?

_____

_____

_____

_____

The trek from Dothan to Egypt was approximately 300 miles. If all went well, Joseph probably walked twenty miles per day for fifteen days. That would have been a long time for him to think about his brothers' actions—a long time for anger to fester. Then Joseph arrived in Egypt—alone in a pagan society with foreign customs and a foreign language. Read Genesis 39:1–18. What happened to Joseph in his boss's home? How did his boss react (see verses 19–20)?

_____

_____

_____

MYplace O BIBLE STUDY

Read Genesis 40:12–15, 23. How were Joseph's hopes for release dashed?

_____

_____

_____

Human reasoning would say God abandoned Joseph. But that's not true. Read Genesis 39:2–3, 21, 23. What do these verses say about God's activity in Joseph's circumstances?

_____

_____

_____

Compare these verses with Psalm 105:16–20. What was God doing in Joseph's life while he was in prison? Why did God do this? (Read Genesis 41:37–41 for the answer.)

_____

_____

_____

Eventually, Joseph and his brothers were reunited. Joseph could have sought revenge at this point, but he didn't. Read Genesis 50:19–21. What did he do instead?

_____

_____

_____

What did Joseph's attitude and behavior show he thought about God's character (see verse 20)?

_____

_____

_____

Read Romans 8:28. When you trust that God is sovereign over every detail of your life, it will enable you to forgive the person who appears responsible for your taking an unwelcome detour. With forgiveness comes wholeness and freedom mentally, emotionally, spiritually, and physically. How have you seen God redeem hardship—largely caused by someone else—for your good and His glory?

_____

_____

_____

> *Sovereign God, I invite Your involvement in every detail of my life to bring Your eternal purposes to pass. Amen.*

— DAY 3: I REST MY CASE

Father God, sometimes I wish I could take matters into my own hands when I'm wronged. I give You my desire to get even, and I choose to trust Your justice system instead. Amen.

Here's one of the best pieces of counsel I've ever received: "Forgiving your offender is more readily possible when you understand God will hold him accountable for what he's done. But remember—He will hold you accountable for your response." I've applied this wisdom many times, and it works.

We might experience hurtful situations in which we never know the identity of our offender. I felt angry when an intruder broke into our home and stole several pieces of jewelry to which I was emotionally attached. Knowing that God would someday serve justice helped me forgive the mystery man, and my anger dissipated.

We might experience pain from someone who never asks our forgiveness. Again, knowing God will hold that person accountable frees us from the possibility of being enslaved to anger, the gnawing desire for personal revenge, and negative behaviors we adopt in a futile attempt to heal our hurts. Read Jeremiah 17:10. What does the Lord do that we cannot? Why is this necessary for justice to be fair?

_____

_____

_____

How might justice look if we assumed the role of judge?

_____

_____

_____

Our natural bent wants justice served *immediately* if not sooner. Read Deuteronomy 32:35. What three-word phrase describes God's perspective? What does this mean to you?

_____

_____

_____

Compare with Proverbs 20:22. What does this verse tell you not to do? What does it say your attitude is to be?

_____

_____

_____

In the *New Living Translation,* this verse reads, "Wait for the LORD to handle the matter." What is your natural tendency when God's handling of the matter takes longer than you wish or doesn't seem fair to you?

_____

_____

_____

Now read Psalm 94. How did the writer feel (see verses 3, 17)?

_____

_____

_____

Write out verse 19. Circle the word that says what filled his mind. Underline the words that describe what overcame the negative effect of his doubts.

_____

_____

_____

In what truths did the writer find consolation (see verses 13–15, 18, 22–23)?

Sometimes the offense is a legal matter. Read Romans 13:4. How has God covered that base on your behalf? How might trusting God for justice enable you to experience inner freedom even if the court system appears to fail you?

The Bible contains numerous commands about how to treat your offender. Some say what *not* to do; others say what *to* do. Read the following verses and fill in the appropriate boxes.

VERSE:	WHAT ARE YOU TO DO?	WHAT ARE YOU NOT TO DO?
Leviticus 19:18		
Luke 6:27-28		
Romans 12:19-20		
1 Peter 3:9		

WEEK TEN FORGIVENESS: WHAT IT IS, WHAT IT IS NOT

Read 1 Peter 2:21–23. What was Christ's response when others caused Him pain?

_____

_____

_____

You are to follow in Christ's steps. With whom should you to rest your case? What truth gives you the ability to do as Jesus did?

_____

_____

_____

Heavenly Father, I trust You to do what is right when someone hurts me, and I trust You to help me respond in a way that reflects Your nature. Amen.

— DAY 4: EXPOSING THE MYTHS ABOUT FORGIVENESS

Dear Father, forgiving an offender can be so difficult. Thank You for giving me guiding principles by which to succeed. Amen.

We often suppose our assumptions about forgiveness are based on truth, but that is not always the case. Today, you will look at several common beliefs that, in reality, have no biblical basis.

The first faulty belief is that forgiveness means forgetting the offense happened. Our human brains cannot wipe their hard drives clean, so "forgive and forget" is impossible. Does this mean we can never truly forgive because we never actually forget what happened? No.

Read Philippians 3:12–14. Paul uses the words "forgetting the past," but this doesn't mean deleting your memory bank. It means "refusing to dwell" on the past. What actions can you take to not dwell on a past offense (see verse 13)?

_____

_____

_____

A second faulty belief is that *forgiveness guarantees reconciliation*. The Bible never promises restored relationships. We can't control our offender's response, and sometimes allowing that person back into our lives isn't safe. Sometimes trust must be re-established. We need godly wisdom to know when to set healthy boundaries and what they should be.

If restoration does happen, it can take a long time, and the relationship will rarely look like it did before the offense. In some cases, that might be a good thing. Regardless, we need to do what is right, and we need to be willing to embrace a new normal. Read Colossians 3:12–15. What characteristics are you to demonstrate even if the relationship doesn't heal as you wish it would?

_____

_____

_____

A third faulty belief is that *forgiveness is a one-time event*. Have you ever forgiven someone but felt the offense's sting again, and again, and again? Forgiveness is like peeling an onion one layer at a time. It's a process. Each time you feel the sting, you give your pain back to Jesus and ask Him to help you forgive again. Read Romans 8:29. What is God's desired outcome for you?

_____

_____

_____

Read Malachi 3:3. A refiner's fire neither destroys nor consumes; it burns away the dross and leaves pure precious metal behind. As God removes layers of shame, anger, blame, and mistrust in your heart, you become more like Jesus. Write a prayer of surrender below, inviting Him to continue the process of making you more like Christ even though it hurts.

_____

_____

_____

A fourth faulty belief is that *forgiveness is for the offender's benefit*. To forgive is to actually "send away" the offender for God to deal with the person. We open our clenched fists and release the offender and the negative emotions we feel toward him or her. As we do, we are able to receive the peace and joy that comes from obeying God's command to forgive our enemies. Read Psalm 32:1–5. How would you apply this passage to what happens when you confess anger and bitterness and unforgiveness?

_____

_____

_____

God, guard me from faulty perceptions about forgiveness and guide me in Your truth. Amen.

— DAY 5: PRAY FOR YOUR ENEMIES

Jesus, You prayed for Your enemies. Show me how to do that in a positive way. Amen.

Jesus' teachings revealed the vast difference between man's thoughts and God's. Read Matthew 5:44. Write this verse using one color for man's thoughts and a different color for God's thoughts. According to this verse, what is man's typical response toward his enemies?

_____

_____

_____

_____

What does God say your response should be?

_____

_____

_____

_____

We might consider our enemies to be the people who cut us off on the freeway, post a nasty comment on our Facebook page, or zip into the parking stall we had planned to use. But the Jews faced enemies of a different sort. From Egyptian slave masters to the Roman Empire, their enemies tortured and killed them. Jesus telling His audience to pray for them was similar to telling present-day Middle Eastern believers to pray for ISIS.

Some people may find that praying for their enemies comes naturally: "God, rain fire down from heaven on them! Burn their crops. Dry up their water supply. Make them miserable!" But when the Bible tells us to pray on our enemies' behalf, it has something different—something better—than this in mind.

Praying for our enemies means interceding for them before the heavenly Father who knows our hearts and motives. It means caring enough about them to spend time and energy seeking their good. Anyone can pray for brimstone to fall on their adversaries, but only pure hearts can stand before God and pray for the good of those bent on their destruction. Read Luke 23:34. Who spoke these words? On what occasion?

What did Jesus pray?

Compare with Acts 7:57–60. Who spoke these words? On what occasion?

What did Stephen pray?

Read Ephesians 6:10–12. How are we to fight a spiritual battle (see verses 10–11)?

_____

_____

_____

We fight spiritual battles with spiritual weapons, and praying truth is one of them. Read Proverbs 8:32–36, 21:21, John 3:19–21, 8:32, Romans 12:2, and 1 John 1:9. Choose three verses and write prayers applicable to your situation based on the truth they contain. Here is an example:

> Proverbs 2:1–5—"Father, I pray that _____ will value and thirst for wisdom and understanding. Teach her to search for them as for a hidden treasure. Use that search to draw her to Yourself. May she discover the knowledge of who You are, and may that discovery change her life. Amen."

Praying for our enemies' good requires obedience, and God honors those who do what He says. Read John 14:21. What amazing blessing do the obedient in heart experience?

_____

_____

_____

_____

Praying for our enemies is our responsibility. Changing their hearts is the Holy Spirit's role. He also changes us by aligning our thoughts about our enemies with His thoughts about them. Syncing our thoughts with His means living from the truth rather than from lies. It means experiencing freedom from anger and unforgiveness and the destructive behaviors they bring. It means experiencing wholeness and healing emotionally, mentally, spiritually, and physically. It means we will flourish—and that's what God has created us to do.

> *Father, grant me an obedient heart to pray with genuine concern for my enemies' good so that I might experience You and the life for which You've created me. Amen.*

— DAY 6: REFLECTION AND APPLICATION

Lord, my health has suffered from choices I've made, and I feel badly. Help me not to languish in guilt and shame but to move forward in freedom and anticipation of good things to come. Amen.

The food-related choices I made caused me to reach a scary unhealthy weight for my frame. This, combined with poor choices I made related to exercise, cause me to suffer chronic pain for years. But rather than acknowledging faulty thinking and changing my behaviors, I assumed things could never improve and sought comfort in food. As I stated earlier, I eventually suffered leg injuries that resulted in a loss of mobility for three months.

Two weeks after starting to walk again, I broke into shingles. My body was crying for help. I had taken it for granted and neglected its care. In desperation, it finally said, "Enough."

I sometimes wonder what opportunities I missed during those years. Even more, I regret how my example as a ministry leader mislead others. I told audiences that Christ could heal their wounds, empower them to say no to temptation, and enable them to live as overcomers, but my actions reflected a different message. I portrayed a double standard, and my example may have hindered others from experiencing freedom. For that I am sorry.

My First Place for Health journey has included learning to own responsibility for my choices and their effect on my physical, mental, emotional, and spiritual well-being. I understand now that no one can care for my body but me, and doing so requires intentionality. There are no shortcuts, and I'm now committed to the long haul.

My journey has also included learning to extend grace to myself as I would to others who are walking a similar path. I could beat myself up for past failures and wasted years, but doing so would not profit me in any way. So instead, I choose to give thanks daily for the gift of restored health and the opportunities it brings.

If I fall short of my new goals on any given day, I refuse to linger in the shadow of shame and guilt. Instead, I walk in the light of truth of verses such as Psalm 103:8–18. God's love never fails. He's slow to anger and does not constantly accuse us of failure as Satan does. He understands our weaknesses and extends His salvation toward us.

Can you relate to my experience? In keeping with this week's focus on forgiveness, learn to forgive yourself for the choices you've made. Our natural mindset is to linger on the failures, but instead choose to focus on God's mercy and grace toward you. He extends grace to you as you grow in every aspect of your life, so do the same for yourself.

> *Father God, thank You for Your grace in my life. Help me not to focus on past failure but to forgive myself and move forward by faith to the destiny for which You created me. Amen.*

— DAY 7: REFLECTION AND APPLICATION

Dear God, my mind so easily believes lies. Grant me the discernment to recognize untrue thoughts when they come. Amen.

God is forgiving by nature, so He forgives us when we confess our sins to Him. Because He forgives, we are commanded to forgive those who hurt us. If only it were that easy to do.

WEEK TEN FORGIVENESS: WHAT IT IS, WHAT IT IS NOT

At the moment we experience emotional wounding, Satan sneaks in and plants lies in our minds. Often, we don't recognize these untruths for what they really are—his insidious way of trying to destroy us. And because we fail to identify them, we entertain them and begin to believe them as truth. Eventually we act on them.

Our ability to forgive and experience God's blessing for obedience rises and falls on our thoughts. So let's make sure we're thinking truth. Read 1 Peter 5:8. The writer warned us to be of a sober mind—to think clearly, to stay focused, and to be intentional about the thoughts we entertain. He understood Satan wants to taint and twist our minds because our thoughts determine the direction our lives take and ultimately our eternal destiny.

The following are a few examples lies Satan wants you to believe. Beneath each one, write down the truth based on the Bible reference given. Here is a sample:

Untruth: This pain is all my fault.

Truth: (Psalm 14:3): *This pain is the result of sin and unresolved issues in the offender's life. Perhaps I have unresolved issues as well.*

Untruth: The hurt I've experienced has ruined me forever.

Truth: (Jeremiah 29:11):

Untruth: I must be a horrible person for others to treat me this way. No one loves me.

Truth: (Romans 8:37-39):

Untruth: There is no way I can ever forgive this person for the pain she has caused.
Truth: (Philippians 4:13):

Untruth: My offender doesn't deserve my forgiveness.
Truth: (Romans 5:8):

What other lies has Satan fed you to make forgiving your offenders difficult?

Untruth:

Truth:

WEEK TEN   FORGIVENESS: WHAT IT IS, WHAT IT IS NOT

Untruth:

Truth:

Untruth:

Truth:

Identifying these lies will come more easily as you know the Truth. Knowing the Truth comes by spending time reading it and listening to it. My friend, God, is crazy in love with you. His intent toward you is always for good, because He is good and cannot do anything contrary to His nature. He will never ask you to do something that is impossible apart from His power in you. So, when God asks you to release an offender to Him and leave justice in His hands, rest assured that you can do it.

> *Lord Jesus, You are truth personified. Draw me closer to You that I might more readily identify the enemy's lies and tactics. I love You. Thank You for loving me. Amen.*

WEEK ELEVEN: REVIEW AND REFLECT

To help you shape your short victory celebration testimony, work through the following questions in your prayer journal, one on each day leading up to your group's celebration:

DAY ONE: List some of the benefits you have gained by allowing the Lord to transform your life through this First Place for Health session. Be mindful that He has been active in all four aspects of your being, so list benefits you have received in the physical, mental, emotional and spiritual realms.

DAY TWO: In what ways have you most significantly changed *mentally*? Have you seen a shift in the ways you think about yourself, food, your relationships or God? How has Scripture memory been a part of these shifts?

DAY THREE: In what ways have you most significantly changed *emotionally*? Have you begun to identify how your feelings influence your relationship to food and exercise? What are you doing to stay aware of your emotions, both positive and negative?

DAY FOUR: In what ways have you most significantly changed *spiritually*? How has your relationship with God deepened? How has drawing closer to Him made a difference in the other three areas of your life?

DAY FIVE: In what ways have you most significantly changed *physically*? Have you met or exceeded your weight/measurement goals? How has your health improved?

DAY SIX: Was there one person in your First Place for Health group who was particularly encouraging to you? How did their kindness make a difference in your First Place for Health journey?

DAY SEVEN: Summarize the previous six questions into a one-page testimony, or "faith story," to share at your group's victory celebration.

WEEK TWELVE: A TIME TO CELEBRATE!

Join your group in celebrating the benefits you have gained, the shift in the way you see yourself, how your relationship with God has changed, and the improvement in your health. Spend time celebrating your group and the encouragement you have experienced through each other. Celebrate!

LEADER DISCUSSION GUIDE

— WEEK ONE: THE POWER OF THE MIND

Discuss how our thoughts impact us mentally, physically, spiritually, and emotionally. Invite group members to tell how they have experienced this to be true.

Discuss the quote, "Watch your thoughts, for they become words. Watch your words, for they become actions. Watch your actions, for they become habits. Watch your habits, for they become character. Watch your character, for it becomes your destiny." Ask your group members for an example of how they have seen this prove true.

Ask someone to read Genesis 3:1. Draw attention to the serpent's question: "Did God really say, 'You must not eat from any tree in the garden?'" Compare with Genesis 2:16. Discuss how Satan can twist God's words in our minds to cause us to doubt and sin. Ask for examples of how he does this today.

Ask someone to read Romans 8:6. Discuss the contrast between the two minds mentioned here—one being death, and the other being life and peace. Now read Isaiah 26:3. Note the word stayed implies "being focused on." Invite your group to share personal examples of when they experienced peace in a difficult situation. Ask how their thoughts played a role in their knowing peace.

Read 1 Peter 1:13, focusing on the command to prepare our minds for action. Ask to what action this might refer. Talk about the need to be prepared for trials and challenges so we are ready to face them when they strike.

Discuss how Scripture memorization plays a vital role in preparing us for spiritual battle. Invite your group to share strategies for memorizing their weekly verses.

Talk about meditating on God's Word—what it means and how to do it as you go about your everyday life. What impact has God's Word had on the group's wellness habits?

Discuss what happens at night when we can't sleep. Sometimes we pray, but sometimes we lie awake as our minds flit from one anxious thought to another. Read Psalm 63:6–8. Describe the psalmist's emotional response as he kept his mind focused on God.

In Ephesians 4:20–24, Paul exhorted believers to put off the old self and put on the new self by being made new in the attitudes of their minds. He then described what that would look like. Split your group into smaller units and assign the following sections: Ephesians 4:25–28; 4:29–32; 5:1–4; and 5:5–11. Ask them to return in a few minutes with the answers to these questions: What behaviors are we to put off? What behaviors are we to demonstrate, and why?

— WEEK TWO: WHAT'S GOD LIKE?

Refer to A.W. Tozer's quote: "What comes into our minds when we think about God is the most important thing about us." Ask your group to identify several mistaken thoughts about God prevalent in our society or within the church and how those thoughts have influenced attitudes and behaviors. Now ask them to contrast those mistaken thoughts with truth. How would applying that truth change lives?

The ultimate revelation of God's character took place on the cross of Calvary. Ask what Jesus' actions declared about God. How did witnessing the crucifixion and the surrounding events impact the centurion's thinking (see Luke 23:47)?

Referring to Day 2, ask someone to read Proverbs 3:2. Discuss how keeping God's commands in our heart brings prosperity. Make sure not to confuse this with the popular "prosperity gospel." Relate it to flourishing in body, soul, mind, and spirit.

Read Romans 8:31–39 aloud as a group. Ask participants to (1) identify evidences of God's love for them based on this passage and (2) make it personal and declare truth by inserting their situation into verses 35 and 37. For instance, someone might say, "Who shall separate me from the love of Christ? Shall the stress I feel from caring for my elderly parents? No, even in this situation, I am more than a conqueror through him who loved me."

Moses sent twelve spies to Canaan (see Numbers 13:26–14:38). When the spies returned, they gave a report of their findings. God had promised Canaan to the Israelites (see 13:1). Ask the group why the ten spies refused to obey Him. How did their incorrect thinking about God influence the masses (see 14:1–4)?

Have someone read Numbers 14:7–9. Compare Joshua and Caleb's attitude to that of the other spies. On what basis did they encourage the people to be bold? Discuss how this truth is relevant to us today. What difference should it make when we face the giants in our lives?

Ask someone to read Numbers 14:11, 27. How does God view a minimized perspective of who He is? Read verse 24. How did God respond to those who understood His trustworthiness? Contrast with Numbers 14:36–37.

Encourage your group to evaluate their thoughts about God. Ask with whom they relate most—the ten spies or Joshua and Caleb. Why?

Ask the group members to share their greatest fear. Encourage them to answer the question, "How would understanding the full measure of God's love conquer that fear?" When those who wish to share have had the opportunity, pray for them using Ephesians 3:14–21.

— WEEK THREE: PRAYER: CONVERSING WITH GOD

Day 1 refers to the importance of giving thanks. Ask someone to read Ephesians 5:18–20. What is the key to being able to give thanks at all times? What is the mind's natural bent apart from the Holy Spirit's control?

Explain that sometimes we wait for what feels like forever for God to answer a specific prayer—like overcoming food's grip or achieving our goal weight. For what can we give thanks when the wait feels too long?

In keeping with the discussion about thanksgiving being a vital element of our prayer lives, invite each member to share (1) a prayer request and (2) one item of thanksgiving related to that request. Take a few moments to pray and thank through these requests.

Explain that praising God shifts our focus from our concerns to the One who's more than able to address them and wants to carry them. Training our minds to meditate on His character qualities including love, wisdom, power, and sovereignty replaces fear with courage. Ask group members to recall a situation when they experienced the power of praise in this way.

First Samuel 2 contains Hannah's praise to God when she fulfilled her promise to leave her little boy in Eli's care. Imagine how difficult that must have been for this woman who had waited so long to bear a child. Refer to this chapter and its context, and then ask someone to read Psalm 50:23. Discuss what offering a sacrifice of praise means.

Day 4 mentioned the Holy Spirit and Jesus interceding on our behalf. Invite someone to read Romans 8:34 and Hebrews 7:25. Explain that sometimes our minds tell us that our prayers aren't spiritual enough for God to hear and answer. How do these verses refute that lie?

Faulty thinking might tell us the only effective prayers are those prayed on our knees for an extended time. But the reality is we lead busy lives. Different life seasons and circumstances bring different responsibilities that can limit the time we might want to spend in focused prayer. So—what do your group members do about that? Ask for tidbits of wisdom they might wish to share. Also ask how the enemy might use this mistaken perception to discourage them from praying altogether.

Note that body posture makes a difference when we pray. Ask someone to read Ephesians 3:14–21. What posture did the writer assume (see verse 14)? What does this posture imply? What caused him to fall to his knees?

Challenge your group members to try a different body posture than is usual for them in the week ahead. If they usually sit, they might kneel. If they usually kneel, they might try walking. If they are able, they might kneel on the floor and pray with their forehead on the ground as though bowing low to the King of heaven. Ask how they might incorporate prayer and praise into their exercise routine.

— WEEK FOUR: REFRAMING OBEDIENCE

Day 1 reflects on God's wisdom. Ask how His creation provides evidences of His wisdom. List several examples, especially pertaining to the human body and how He designed it to function.

Discuss how God's wisdom surpasses our wildest imagination. Why, then, do we often struggle with obeying Him? What is the key to overcoming our desire to do our own thing?

Read Psalm 111:7–8, 10. Compare the New International Version with the New Living Translation, which says, "All he does is just and good, and all his commandments are trustworthy. They are forever true, to be obeyed faithfully and with integrity. . . . Reverence for the Lord is the foundation of true wisdom. The rewards of wisdom come to all who obey him."

Identify a few examples of how God's unchanging laws collide with our changing culture. What promise is given to those who obey His commands even though society says doing so is narrow-minded or old-fashioned?

Psalm 119:55 was mentioned in Day 2. The psalmist wrote that he obeyed God's commands as a result of meditating on His name and character. Discuss the relationship between our view of who God is and our willingness to obey Him. How will we respond to His words if we see Him as an uninvolved God? How will we respond if we have a misperception of His holiness, His omnipresence, or His sovereignty over every detail of our lives?

Obedience requires humility. Read the story of Naaman the leper in 2 Kings 5:9-14. Describe his response to Elisha's instructions. What did this indicate about him? When his officers urged him to do what Elisha said, he came to his senses. What was the outcome?

Compare this to the First Place for Health wellness journey. What instructions are group members given so they might experience wholeness? How does humility help achieve success?

Explain that our obedience and our disobedience affect other people. Eve's story is a prime example. She disobeyed first, and then Adam followed (see Genesis 3:6). Read Romans 5:15, 17-19. Describe the extent to which their sin impacted mankind. Using the same verses, contrast the outcome of their choices with the outcome of Christ's obedience.

Invite the group members to tell about a situation in which they obeyed the Lord and He honored them for it. Invite them also to tell about a situation when they were blessed because another person obeyed God. In other words, they experienced being part of a ripple effect that began when someone said yes to the Lord.

—— WEEK FIVE: WHAT DOES GOD THINK ABOUT ME?

Day 2 focuses on God's love for His children. Ask someone to read Romans 8:31-39. Give group members an opportunity to tell what part of this passage is especially meaningful to them and why.

Read Hebrews 12:5-11. Ask the group what wrong thoughts they might develop when God disciplines them. What could be the root of those misperceptions? What is the truth about God's discipline (see verses 6, 10-11)? How are we to respond (see verses 7, 9)? Why is a correct understanding of God's love for us so vital in the context of responding well?

Read John 13:34–35. What command are we to obey? How does a correct understanding of God's love empower us to do this?

Day 3 focuses on our being transformed. Wrong thinking says there is no hope for change or for overcoming besetting sins and bad habits, but the truth declares something much different. Ask someone to read Colossians 3:1–11. Ask on what basis we find hope for lasting change (see verses 1–4, 10–11). Reread verse 2. What role do our minds play in our transformation? In practical terms, how do we set our minds on things above?

Explain that sometimes we become frustrated or discouraged by slow progress or failure. Ask how the truth of Colossians 3:9–10 brings encouragement. Read these verses in the New Living Translation: "For you have stripped off your old evil nature and all its wicked deeds. In its place you have clothed yourselves with a brand-new nature that is continually being renewed as you learn more and more about Christ, who created this new nature within you."

Invite group members to discuss their feelings about sharing their faith with unbelievers. Many people find the prospect intimidating, or they feel it is best left to the "experts." How does the truth that God appoints us as His ambassadors change their perspective?

At times we grow weary from the inside out, and we forget God's promise to strengthen and empower us. Ask someone to read Isaiah 40:28–31. Discuss God's credibility as our Source of strength (see verse 28). What does God offer to the tired? To the weak (see verse 29)? What does He give to all who wait on Him (see verse 31)?

Tell your group that to "wait on God" means "to be entwined with Him." Ask how we can entwine ourselves with the Lord in the midst of our busy lives.

— WEEK SIX: MOVING FROM FEAR TO FREEDOM

Discuss how fear undermines our efforts to improve our health. For example, we might fear going to the doctor for check-ups because he may tell us we need to lose weight. We might fear going swimming because we feel self-conscious in a bathing suit. We might fear exercising at a gym because we don't know how to use the equipment properly. We might fear being honest about our food struggles because we assume others will judge us.

Day 1 addressed the fear of inadequacy. Ask group members what new activity or endeavor they would attempt if the fear of inadequacy wasn't an issue.

Ask someone to read Hebrews 13:20–21. Encourage participants to focus on the truth that God equips us with everything good to do His will. Invite them to state their needs for doing God's will. Perhaps they need wisdom in their work, patience for parenting, healing from a physical problem, or the ability to forgive an offender. Maybe they need a change in their thinking about the role food plays in their lives, how they view themselves in regard to the number on the scale, or how they care for their body. Take a moment to pray over their requests, thanking God for being faithful to keep His promise.

Day 2 focused on overcoming the fear for our loved ones' well-being. Invite someone to read Exodus 2:1–10, the story of Jochebed. Note that this mother defied the Pharaoh's command to kill all newborn Israelite boys. Discuss the strength and courage she mustered. How was she able to do this?

Unfortunately, our worst fears sometimes come true for our loved ones. Tragedy strikes, and we're left wondering how it could possibly result in anything good. Encourage your group to consider Mary as she watched Jesus die on the cross. Discuss whether she might have wondered the same thing.

When bad things happen to those we love, we might feel as though God has let us down or abandoned us. Read Romans 8:26–27. Discuss what is the truth about what's happening in the spiritual realm on our behalf during such times.

Recite 1 Peter 5:7 aloud several times: "Cast all your anxiety on him because he cares for you." Emphasize a different key word each time. Encourage group members to personalize it by saying, "I will cast all my fear about _____ on You because You care for me."

Everyone experiences life's storms sooner or later. Our thoughts determine our beliefs and ultimately our response. Read Jeremiah 17:7–10. Discuss what promise God gives to those who make Him their hope and confidence. What is an example of wrong thinking when a storm hits? Compare this with the truth of James 1:2–4. How can storms prove to be opportunities?

Close this session with sentence prayers focused on praising God for who He is. No requests—just praise declarations.

— WEEK SEVEN: KEEPING FIRST THINGS FIRST

God wants and deserves top priority in our lives. Read this quote from A.W. Tozer to your group: "To maintain a lifestyle of worship, we must attend to it on a daily basis. If you regulate worship to a once-a-week event, you really do not understand it, and it will take a low priority in your life."[1] Talk about the difference between making worship a Sunday activity and making it a lifestyle. How can wellness endeavors such as making wise food choices, tracking our food, and exercising regularly be considered worship?

Read Proverbs 14:12 to the group: "There is a way that appears to be right, but in the end it leads to death." Discuss how our human bent is to pursue our own desires or follow the path of least resistance, and how those pursuits are often contrary to God's best for us.

Brainstorm with your group to name specific "ways" that seem right but are ultimately harmful. Invite participants to share specific examples related to their health journey.

Ask someone to read Proverbs 8:17–21. Compare the outcome of our own pursuits with the blessings of living according to God's truths.

Day 2 focused on aligning our thoughts with God's thoughts in the context of loving others. Read James 1:27. Ask the group what this verse teaches about God's values. How can we share those values in practical ways?

Note that we are to demonstrate Christ's mindset in our relationships (see Philippians 2:5). Ask participants to describe what Christ's mindset looked like based on His interactions with people. Invite discussion about practical ways we can mirror the same.

God commands us to make gaining wisdom a priority. Read Proverbs 4:4–13. Discuss the connection between gaining wisdom and growing in personal holiness.

Time is precious. Mention that exercise being a time-waster is a common misperception. Link this back to Proverbs 14:12. What is the result of such thinking? What does reframing that mindset look like?

Have someone read Micah 6:8. Focus on the third of God's requirements: that we walk humbly with Him. Ask the group members to define humility. What is the connection between humility and effectively making God's priorities our own?

WEEK EIGHT: WHEN LIFE IS HARD

Day 1 referred to peace in the midst of adversity. Share one of your favorite Bible verses that brings you peace. Invite your group to do the same.

At some point in life, we might encounter a trial that feels impossibly big. Perhaps our thoughts say, *Even God can't fix this one.* Some of your group members might feel this way about their weight loss goals or obsession with food. Assign four people to read the following verses, one immediately following the other, with no discussion between them: Psalm 34:4, 6, 17, 19. When they have finished reading, discuss the common thread woven throughout. Focus on the truth that with God all things are possible.

Day 2 addressed a question with which many people wrestle when they experience adversity: "Is God punishing me for doing something wrong?" Ask someone to read 1 Peter 4:19. Discuss the possibility of our pain being a natural consequence to poor choices, but focus on the truth that God allows suffering to purify and strengthen us. Trials are often the portal to knowing Him more intimately.

First Peter 4:19 tells us to commit ourselves to our faithful Creator. Ask the group how that name for God relates to us in our suffering. Note that we are called to continue doing good even as we suffer, which seems contrary to human nature. What incorrect thoughts might try to derail us from obeying this command?

Ask someone to read Daniel 3:14–18. Discuss the men's response: "We know our God is able to save us. But even if He doesn't, we won't worship idols or this image." How does this response demonstrate entrusting our lives to our faithful Creator? Invite participants to make this truth personal by filling in the blank with their situation: "God is able to _____ . But even if He doesn't, I will continue to worship Him only."

Day 4 asked whether God cares about us in our suffering. Scripture reassures us of the truth that He is near to the brokenhearted. Invite your group to recall a situation in which God revealed His nearness in their pain.

Some folks think we're disrespectful to ask, "Why, God? Why are You allowing me to suffer like this?" Read Matthew 27:46. Discuss what Jesus meant when He spoke these words. Also discuss how the emotions Jesus felt in this moment show His ability to empathize with us in our pain. How does this knowledge bring comfort?

— WEEK NINE: IT'S NOT ALL ABOUT ME

On Day 1, we noted Samuel's faulty thinking in assuming Eliab would be the next king based on his appearance. To be fair, Samuel may have thought good looks were a prerequisite for kingship because the Lord had chosen Saul—a strikingly handsome young man—as the first king. Ask someone to read 1 Samuel 9:2, 17 to discover what the Bible says about Saul's looks. Then ask someone to read 1 Samuel 17–24. What does this passage reveal about his character? Why would the Lord appoint someone such as this as king over His chosen people?

Have someone read Isaiah 53:2. In the New Living Translation, this verse reads, "There was nothing beautiful or majestic about his appearance, nothing to attract us to him." Ask to whom this verse refers. Note to the group that Jesus may have looked plain or ordinary, but His character certainly was not. Read Isaiah 11:2–5 and describe what He was like.

People in Jesus' day misjudged Him time and time again. Human nature hasn't changed; we still develop opinions and assumptions about others based on what we see. Read Jeremiah 17:10. Discuss how our way of thinking differs from God's in this regard.

Read 1 John 4:9–10. Loving those who hurt us can be costly. Ask the group what price God paid to demonstrate His love for mankind. What might loving our enemies cost us?

Have someone read 1 John 4:11–12. Invite your group members to tell about a time when they witnessed God's love expressed through another person. What happened? How did the experience impact them?

Read 1 John 4:15. Discuss the wonder of God living in us and us in Him. Ask your group for specific examples of how this truth can empower them to change and experience victory in every area of their lives. Ask them what difference this makes in a person's First Place for Health wellness journey.

Ask participants to list dishonoring behaviors and attitudes, but don't linger on them. Summarize the discussion by reading Colossians 3:5–9.

Next, read Colossians 3:10–11. Ask participants to explain how we are clothed in a new nature. Who put it there? How is it renewed on an ongoing basis?

Finally, read Colossians 3:12–15. Ask the group how the qualities listed in this passage bring honor to others. Invite them to tell of an instance when someone demonstrated one of these characteristics toward them and how it made them feel.

On Day 4, we talked about honesty in relationships. Read James 5:16. In this context, James wrote about supporting and praying for those who were physically ill. However, we are four-part persons, and we cannot segregate one part from another. In the First Place for Health Bible study Be Free, Gari Meacham wrote, "Research from Harvard's Medical School's Mind-Body Institute shows that 75–98% of mental, physical, and behavioral illness come from one's thought life."[2] Discuss the negative impact on our well-being when we hide behind secrets and shame, wearing a mask in hopes of impressing others with our spirituality.

— WEEK TEN: FORGIVENESS: WHAT IT IS, WHAT IT IS NOT

Discuss why correct thoughts about God's forgiving nature are vital within the context of our relationships.

Have someone read Proverbs 25:21–22. Invite participants to tell about a situation when they heaped "coals" of kindness on an enemy's head. What did they do? How did the enemy respond? How did the Lord reward them?

Discuss why correct thoughts about God's sovereignty enable us to forgive someone who has changed the course of our lives in a way we wouldn't have chosen.

Read Esther 4:13–17. Discuss Mordecai and Esther's response to the king's edict. How did their behavior demonstrate an understanding of God's sovereignty in their lives?

Day 4 focused on myths about forgiveness. Another false belief is that we should wait until the offender asks for forgiveness before we forgive. Billy Graham addressed that myth when he wrote, "Don't come to the end of your life and look back with regret over a hurt that could have been forgiven or a relationship that could have been healed—if you had only seized the initiative and taken the first step."[3] Ask what hinders us from taking the first step.

Invite participants to share a time when either they took the first step and forgave their offender (whether or not the offender was even aware they did it) or someone else took the first step and offered them forgiveness. How did the story end?

Day 5 addressed praying for one's enemies. Invite group members to read the Scripture-based prayers they wrote. Ask if they have other verses they would like to share for everyone's benefit.

Day 5 also mentioned fighting spiritual battles. Encourage participants to ask the Lord to reveal the root of their offender's behavior for the purpose of praying for that root issue to be removed. Note that if that issue is not removed, praying over symptoms is like slapping a bandage on an infection and thinking it will heal the problem.

Encourage participants to ask God for insights about their offender's attitudes and behaviors. Is the person dealing with stress at home or on the job? What is the person's health condition? Has he or she experienced woundedness in the past? If so, has he or she ever dealt with it appropriately?

Note to the group it is helpful to remember that hurting people hurt people. Trying to understand where they are coming from develops empathy in us. Who knows but that softening in our heart toward them might help reconciliation happen?

— WEEK ELEVEN: REVIEW AND REFLECT

Be creative with your Victory Celebration. Remember you're celebrating what God has accomplished during your group's 12-week session. Spend time celebrating your group and the encouragement you have experienced through each other. Give each member an opportunity to share their review and reflection. Celebrate the successes and milestones accomplished. See the "Planning a Victory Celebration" in *My Place for Leadership*.

FIRST PLACE FOR HEALTH
JUMP START MENUS

This week of recipes is based on approximately 1,300 to 1,400 calories per day, allowing for snack or dessert options up to 200 calories per day. All recipe and menu nutritional information was determined using the MasterCook software, a program that accesses a database containing more than 6,000 food items prepared using the United States Department of Agriculture (USDA) publications and information from food manufacturers. As with any nutritional program, MasterCook calculates the nutritional values of the recipes based on ingredients. Nutrition may vary due to how the food is prepared, where the food comes from, soil content, season, ripeness, processing and method of preparation. For these reasons, please use the recipes and menu plans as approximate guides. As always, consult your physician and/or a registered dietitian before starting a weight-loss program.

For those who need more calories,
add the following to the 1,400–1,500 calorie plan:

1,500-1,600 calories:	1 oz.-eq. of protein, 1 oz.-eq. grains, ½ cup vegetables, 1 tsp. healthy oils
1,700-1,800 calories:	1½ oz.-eq. of protein, 2 oz.-eq. grains, 1 cup of vegetables, 1 tsp. healthy oils
1,900-2,000 calories:	2 oz.-eq. of protein, 2 oz.-eq. of grains, 1 cup vegetables, ½ cup fruit, 1 tsp. healthy oils
2,100-2,200 calories:	3 oz.-eq. of protein, 3 oz.-eq. grains, 1½ cup vegetables, ½ cup fruit, 2 tsp. healthy oils
2,300-2,400 calories:	4 oz.-eq. of protein, 4 oz.-eq. of grains, 2 cups vegetables 3 cups frit, 3 tsp. healthy oils

-

DAY 1 | BREAKFAST

Quickie Bacon and Eggs

1 slice Canadian bacon

2 eggs

Preheat oven to 350° F. Place slice of Canadian bacon in cup of muffin tin. Scramble eggs with salt and pepper, to taste. Pour into tin with bacon (may need to press bacon into tin while pouring). Bake in oven for 15 minutes or until eggs are set. (Tip: Make enough for the week and just warm in microwave before serving.) Serves 1.

Serve with: ½ cup fruit and toasted English muffin (adds 2 oz.-eq grain and ½ cup fruit).

Nutritional Information: 193 calories; 12g fat (57.7% calories from fat); 18g protein; 1g carbohydrate; 0g dietary fiber; 438mg cholesterol; 539mg sodium.

Live It Tracker: 2½ oz.-eq. protein.

DAY 1 | LUNCH

Grown-Up Grilled Cheese

cooking spray

1 cup sliced red onion

1 large garlic clove, minced

1 cup shredded reduced-fat sharp white cheddar cheese

8 1½-oz. hearty whole-grain bread, sliced

2 cups fresh spinach leaves

8 sliced tomato

6 slices center-cut bacon, cooked

Heat a large nonstick skillet over medium-low heat. Coat pan with cooking spray. Add 1 cup onion and garlic; cook for 10 minutes or until tender and golden brown, stirring occasionally. Sprinkle 2 tablespoons cheese over each of 4 bread slices. Top each slice with ½ cup spinach, 2 tomato slices, 2 tablespoons onion mixture, and 1½ bacon slices. Sprinkle each bread slice with 2 tablespoons cheese; top with the remaining 4 slices. Heat skillet over medium heat. Coat pan with cooking spray. Place sandwiches in pan and cook for 3 minutes on each side or until golden brown and cheese melts. Serves 4.

Serve with: 1 cup carrot sticks and 2 tablespoons lowfat ranch dressing (adds 1 cup vegetable).

Nutritional Information: 377 calories; 11g fat (25.0% calories from fat); 21g protein; 54g carbohydrate; 9g dietary fiber; 14mg cholesterol; 802mg sodium.

Live It Tracker: 1½ oz. eq. protein, 2½ oz.-eq. grains, 1 cup vegetables.

DAY 1 | DINNER

Balsamic Chicken with Avocado

Balsamic Dressing:
- 1/3 cup balsamic vinegar
- ¼ cup olive oil
- 2 tbsp. water
- 2 tsp. Italian seasoning
- 2 tsp. minced garlic
- 1 tsp. honey
- ½ tsp. salt
- 4 skinless and boneless chicken breast fillets

Salad:
- 4 slices bacon, diced and trimmed of all fat
- 8 cups mixed salad lettuce greens
- 2 tomatoes, chopped
- 1 red onion, thinly sliced
- 1 avocado, sliced
- ¼ cup crumbled feta cheese
- salt and pepper, to taste

Whisk balsamic dressing ingredients together until well combined. Pour 2 to 3 tablespoons into a shallow bowl. Add the chicken thighs and coat evenly. Season with salt and pepper; set aside for 10 minutes while frying the bacon. Fry bacon until crisp in a skillet over medium-high heat. Clean pan with paper towel. Cook chicken fillets until cooked through (about 15 minutes). Arrange all salad greens in a large bowl. Top with the bacon, chicken, and avocado, and sprinkle with feta, extra Italian seasoning, if desired, and salt and pepper, to taste. Drizzle with the remaining dressing and serve. Serves 4.

Nutritional Information: 501 calories; 31g fat (54.2% calories from fat); 42g protein; 17g carbohydrate; 5g dietary fiber; 108mg cholesterol; 576mg sodium.

Live It Tracker: 4 oz.-eq. protein; 2 cups vegetables; ½ cup fruit.

DAY 2 | BREAKFAST

Banana Oatmeal Muffins

¼ cup peanut butter

1 egg

¼ cup maple syrup

3 medium ripe bananas

2 small zucchinis (2 cups grated; don't squeeze water out)

½ cup lowfat milk

1 tsp. vanilla

3 cups old-fashioned oats

1 tbsp. baking powder

1 tsp. cinnamon

¼ tsp. salt

Preheat oven to 375° F. Spray a muffin tin with cooking spray. Place bananas in a large bowl and mash with a fork. Add peanut butter, maple syrup, milk, vanilla, and egg, stirring to combine. Add oats, baking powder, cinnamon, and salt. Stir until just combined. Spoon mixture into muffin cups, filling to the top. Bake for 25 minutes or until a toothpick comes out clean. Store cooled oatmeal muffins in an air-tight container in the refrigerator. (These freeze well.) Add ¼ cup of mini chocolate chips for added flavor, if desired. Serves 16.

Serve with: 1½ cups lowfat milk and 1 cup fruit (adds 1½ cup dairy and 1 cup fruit).

Nutritional Information: 128 calories; 3g fat (23.5% calories from fat); 5g protein; 21g carbohydrate; 3g dietary fiber; 13mg cholesterol; 154mg sodium.

Live It Tracker: ½ oz. eq. protein; ½ cup of fruit.

DAY 2 | LUNCH

Turkey Cranberry Wrap

3 cups cooked, shredded turkey (or chicken) (leftover or deli turkey works well in this recipe)

½ cup almonds, whole or sliced

2 stalks celery, chopped

2–3 tbsp. light mayonnaise (or Greek yogurt), to taste

½ cup cranberry sauce (or dried cranberries)

salt and freshly ground pepper, to taste

4 large tortillas

Combine all ingredients together in a bowl. Season with salt and pepper. Spoon filling into tortillas and roll into a wrap. Serves 4.

Serve with: 1 serving baked chips, 1 cup veggie sticks with 2 tablespoons ranch dressing, and an apple (adds 1½ cup vegetables and 1 cup fruit).

Nutritional Information: 428 calories; 16g fat (32.4% calories from fat); 29g protein; 45g carbohydrate; 5g dietary fiber; 59mg cholesterol; 496mg sodium.

Live It Tracker: ½ oz.-eq. protein; 3 oz.-eq. grains.

DAY 2 | DINNER

Easy Tortellini Soup with Spinach

1 tbsp. olive oil

3 cloves garlic, minced

1 onion, diced

4 cups chicken broth

1 (14.5-oz.) can petite diced tomatoes, undrained

1 (9-oz.) package refrigerated three-cheese tortellini

½ tsp. dried basil

½ tsp. dried oregano

1 bay leaf

kosher salt and freshly ground black pepper, to taste

3 cups baby spinach, chopped

2 tbsp. grated Parmesan

Heat 1 tablespoon olive oil in a large stockpot over medium heat. Add garlic and onion and cook, stirring frequently, until onions have become translucent (about 2 to 3 minutes). Stir in chicken broth, diced tomatoes, tortellini, basil, oregano, bay leaf, and 1 cup water; season with salt and pepper, to taste. Bring to a boil; reduce heat and simmer until tortellini is cooked through (about 5 to 6 minutes). Stir in spinach until it begins to wilt (about 2 minutes). Serve immediately, garnished with Parmesan. Serves 4.

Serve with: 9 crackers or 4-inch slice of French bread (adds 1 grain).

Nutritional Information: 169 calories; 7g fat (37.3% calories from fat); 11g protein; 16g carbohydrate; 2g dietary fiber; 17mg cholesterol; 918mg sodium.

Live It Tracker: 1 oz.-eq. protein; ½ oz.-eq. grains; 1 cup vegetables.

DAY 3 | BREAKFAST

Peanut Butter and Jelly Wafflewich

2 whole-grain frozen waffles
1 tbsp. peanut butter
1 tbsp. all-fruit jelly

Toast waffles. Spread with peanut butter and jelly. Serves 1.

Serve with: ½ cup mixed fruit and 1½ cups lowfat milk (adds ½ cup fruit and 1½ cups dairy).

Nutritional Information: 232 calories; 11g fat (41.5% calories from fat); 6g protein; 30g carbohydrate; 2g dietary fiber; 3mg cholesterol; 272mg sodium.

Live It Tracker: ½ oz.-eq. protein; 2 oz.-eq. grains.

DAY 3 | LUNCH

Ham and Swiss with Pear Sandwich

2 slices low-sodium deli ham
1 slice swiss cheese
½ pear, sliced thin
1 tsp. honey mustard

Assemble sandwich. Serves 1.

Serve with: 1 serving of fruit.

Nutritional Information: 307 calories; 7g fat (19.7% calories from fat); 43g protein; 17g carbohydrate; 2g dietary fiber; 70mg cholesterol; 1123mg sodium.

Live It Tracker: 4 oz-eq protein; ½ cup fruit.

DAY 3 | DINNER

Bean and Cheese Nachos

1 15-oz. can refried black beans

8 oz. 90% lean ground sirloin

½ tsp. chili powder

4 green onions, thinly sliced

8 (6-inch) corn tortillas, cut into wedges

cooking spray

2/3 cup fat-free evaporated milk, divided

1½ tsp. cornstarch

2 oz. preshredded reduced-fat cheddar cheese (about ½ cup)

¼ cup light sour cream

1/3 cup tomato, chopped

¼ cup fresh cilantro, coarsely chopped

½ tsp. kosher salt

Preheat broiler. Heat a large nonstick skillet over medium-high. Add beef; cook 8 minutes, stirring to crumble. Stir in chili powder. Stir in beans and green onions; cook 1 minute. Remove pan from heat. Arrange tortilla wedges in a single layer on a large foil-lined baking sheet coated with cooking spray. Coat tortillas with cooking spray. Broil 2 minutes on each side or until lightly browned and crisp. Remove pan from oven. Spoon beef mixture evenly over tortillas. Combine ¼ cup milk and cornstarch in a bowl, stirring with a whisk. Combine cornstarch mixture and remaining milk in a small saucepan over medium-high; bring to a simmer. Stir in cheese; cook 2 minutes or until smooth, stirring frequently. Combine remaining 2 tablespoons water and sour cream. Drizzle cheese mixture and sour cream mixture over nachos. Top with tomato, cilantro, and salt. Serves 4.

Serve with: ½ cup of salsa.

Nutritional Information: 451 calories; 16g fat (30.8% calories from fat); 27g protein; 52g carbohydrate; 9g dietary fiber; 48mg cholesterol; 941mg sodium.

Live It Tracker: 2 oz.-eq. protein; 3 oz.-eq. grains; ½ cup vegetables; ½ cup dairy.

DAY 4 | BREAKFAST

Baked Breakfast Taquitos

10 corn tortillas, softened

3 large eggs, scrambled

6 oz. spicy lowfat Italian sausage, crumbled

¼ cup julienned sun dried tomatoes, drained

1 avocado, halved, seeded, peeled, and diced

1 cup shredded sharp cheddar cheese

Preheat oven to 425° F. Line a baking sheet with parchment paper; set aside. Working one at a time, transfer tortilla to a work surface; place eggs, sausage, sun dried tomatoes, avocado and cheddar cheese in the center of each wrapper. Bring the bottom edge of the tortilla tightly over the filling, rolling from bottom to top until the top of the tortilla is reached. Repeat with remaining tortilla and filling. Place taquitos seam-side down onto prepared baking sheet. Bake until taquitos are crisp and cheese has melted (about 12 to 15 minutes). Serves 10.

Serve with: ½ cup of salsa and 1 cup of orange juice (adds 1 cup fruit).

Nutritional Information: 218 calories; 14g fat (58.0% calories from fat); 9g protein; 14g carbohydrate; 2g dietary fiber; 88mg cholesterol; 284mg sodium.

Live It Tracker: 1 oz.-eq. of protein; 1 oz.-eq. of grains.

DAY 4 | LUNCH

Greek Pita

½ whole-wheat pita

1 cup Romaine lettuce

¼ cup feta cheese

¼ cup chickpeas

½ cucumber, sliced

¼ small red onion, sliced

1 tbsp. Greek dressing

Assemble salad. Serves 1.

Serve with: 8 whole-grain pita chips (adds 1 grain).

Nutritional Information: 392 calories; 12g fat (26.0% calories from fat); 19g protein; 55g carbohydrate; 11g dietary fiber; 33mg cholesterol; 807mg sodium.

Live It Tracker: 1½ oz.-eq. protein; 3 oz.-eq. grains; 1 cup vegetables.

DAY 4 | DINNER

Pork Chops with Honey and Lemon Sauce

- 4 bone-in pork loin chops
- ¼ cup lemon juice
- ¼ cup honey
- 2 tbsp. reduced-sodium soy sauce
- 1 garlic clove, minced

In a large nonstick skillet coated with cooking spray, cook pork chops over medium heat until a thermometer reads 145° F (approximately 5 to 6 minutes on each side). Remove; let stand 5 minutes. Combine remaining ingredients; add to pan. Cook over medium heat 3 to 4 minutes, stirring occasionally. Serve with chops. Serves 4.

Serve with: 1 cup roasted broccoli and a side salad (adds 1½ cups vegetables).

Nutritional Information: 202 calories; 5g fat (22.8% calories from fat); 20g protein; 20g carbohydrate; trace dietary fiber; 47mg cholesterol; 340mg sodium.

Live It Tracker: 2½ oz.-eq. protein.

DAY 5 | BREAKFAST

Smoothie Bowls

2 cups frozen raspberries

2 bananas

½ cup nonfat Greek yogurt

½ cup low fat milk

lowfat granola

In a blender, puree the raspberries, bananas, yogurt, and milk until smooth. Divide between bowls and top with sprinkle of granola. Serves 2.

Nutritional Information: 388 calories; 1g fat (2.3% calories from fat); 5g protein; 96g carbohydrate; 14g dietary fiber; 1mg cholesterol; 35mg sodium.

Live It Tracker: 2 cups fruit; ½ cup dairy.

DAY 5 | LUNCH

Simple Cobb Salad

1 cup Romaine lettuce

½ chicken breast, sliced

2 slices cooked turkey bacon

¼ avocado, sliced

1 large boiled egg, sliced

1 tbsp. crumbled blue cheese

1 tbsp. balsamic vinegar

Place salad greens on plate. Add next 5 ingredients and drizzle with balsamic vinegar. Serves 1.

Serve with: whole-grain crackers (adds 1 oz.-eq. grains).

Nutritional Information: 402 calories; 24g fat (52.8% calories from fat); 41g protein; 7g carbohydrate; 2g dietary fiber; 315mg cholesterol; 628mg sodium.

Live It Tracker: 3 oz.-eq. protein; ½ cup vegetables; ½ cup fruit.

DAY 5 | DINNER

Parmesan Crusted Chicken

4 boneless, skinless chicken breast fillets

kosher salt and black pepper

¼ cup panko breadcrumbs

¼ cup grated Parmesan

1 tbsp. olive oil

1 tbsp. fresh flat-leaf parsley, chopped

1 garlic clove, chopped

1 tsp. Dijon mustard

1 lb. cherry tomatoes

Preheat oven to 450° F. Arrange chicken breast fillets on an aluminum foil-lined baking sheet. Season with kosher salt and black pepper. Stir together panko breadcrumbs, grated Parmesan, olive oil, chopped parsley, and chopped garlic clove. Spread Dijon mustard on each chicken breast. Sprinkle with breadcrumb mixture. Arrange cherry tomatoes around chicken. Bake until chicken is just cooked through (14 to 16 minutes). Serve with a side salad and garlic bread. Serves 4.

Serve with: whole-grain roll (adds 1 oz.-eq grains).

Nutritional Information: 350 calories; 8g fat (22.0% calories from fat); 58g protein; 8g carbohydrate; 1g dietary fiber; 141mg cholesterol; 283mg sodium.

Live It Tracker: 4 oz.-eq. protein; 1 cup vegetables.

DAY 6 | BREAKFAST

Baked Steel Cut Oatmeal

¾ cup steel cut oatmeal

½ cup almonds, sliced

1 tsp. baking powder

½ tsp. salt

1 cup blueberries

2 cups lowfat milk

¼ cup maple syrup

1 large egg

3 tbsp. unsalted butter, melted and cooled

2 tsp. vanilla

Preheat oven to 350° F. In an 8-inch baking pan, mix the oats, nuts, baking powder, and salt. Place berries on top. In a medium bowl, whisk the milk, maple syrup, egg, butter, and vanilla. Pour milk mixture over the oat mixture. Bake for 60 minutes or until the top is golden and the oat mixture has set. Serves 4.

Nutritional Information: 379 calories; 20g fat (47.4% calories from fat); 12g protein; 39g carbohydrate; 5g dietary fiber; 78mg cholesterol; 210mg sodium.

Live Tracker: ½ oz.-eq. protein; 1 oz.-eq grains; ½ cup fruit; ½ cup dairy.

DAY 6 | LUNCH

Spicy Ramen

1½ tbsp. reduced-sodium vegetable bouillon paste

¾ cup shredded carrot

¾ cup shiitake mushrooms, sliced

1½ cups baby spinach, chopped

3 hard-boiled eggs, halved

1½ cups cooked ramen noodles

3 tbsp. scallions, sliced

¾ tsp. sesame seeds

3 cups hot water, divided

Place ½ tablespoon bouillon paste, ½ teaspoon miso, ½ teaspoon chili-garlic sauce, and ½ teaspoon ginger in each of 3 pint-and-a-half size canning jars. Layer ¼ cup carrot, ¼ cup mushrooms, ½ cup spinach, 2 egg halves, and ½ cup noodles in each jar. Top each with 1 tablespoon scallions and ¼ teaspoon sesame seeds. Close the jars. Refrigerate for up to 3 days. To make one jar of noodles, add 1 cup of very hot water to one jar. Close the jar and shake to combine. Microwave uncovered on high in 1-minute increments until steaming hot, 2 to 3 minutes. Let stand 5 minutes. Stir before eating. Serves 3.

Nutritional information: 349 calories; 7g fat (16.9% calories from fat); 16g protein; 63g carbohydrate; 9g dietary fiber; 230mg cholesterol; 114mg sodium.

Live It Tracker: 1 oz.-eq. protein; ½ oz.-eq. grains; 1 cup vegetables.

DAY 6 | DINNER

Smothered Chicken

2½ tbsp. vegetable oil

8 3-oz. chicken drumsticks, skin removed

2 sliced bacon, cut into ¼-inch strips

1½ tbsp. all-purpose flour

1 medium onion, thinly sliced

1 garlic clove, thinly sliced

1 large tomato, peeled, seeded, and coarsely chopped

1 tsp. tomato paste

1 cup 2% milk

¼ cup low-sodium chicken broth

2 tsp. parsley, chopped

Preheat oven to 375° F. In an ovenproof nonstick skillet, heat 1 tablespoon of the oil. Season the chicken with salt and pepper and add to the pan. Cook over medium-high heat until browned, about 8 minutes. Transfer the chicken to a plate. Add the bacon to the skillet and cook, stirring, for 2 minutes. Drain fat. Add the remaining 1½ tablespoons of oil to the skillet and stir in the flour until incorporated. Add the onion and garlic and cook over medium heat, stirring until slightly softened. Add the tomato and tomato paste and cook, stirring, for five minutes. Add the milk and broth and bring to a boil, stirring until slightly thickened. Return the chicken and any accumulated juices to the skillet. Cover the chicken and bake in oven for 20 minutes until the meat is cooked through. Remove chicken to plate. Return the skillet to medium heat and cook the gravy, whisking constantly, until smooth (about 2 minutes). Whisk in the chopped parsley, pour the gravy over the chicken legs, and serve. Serves 4.

Serve with: 1 cup green beans, roasted with sea salt, and whole-grain dinner roll (adds 1 cup vegetables and 1 oz.-eq. grains).

Nutritional Information: 339 calories; 21g fat (57.1% calories from fat); 27g protein; 10g carbohydrate; 1g dietary fiber; 100mg cholesterol; 193mg sodium.

Live It Tracker: 3½ oz.-eq. protein; 1 cup vegetables.

DAY 7 | BREAKFAST

Pumpkin Spice Breakfast Cookie

2 cups whole-wheat flour

1 cup old-fashioned oats

1 tsp. baking soda

1 tsp. pumpkin pie spice

¼ tsp. salt

1 15-oz. can pumpkin

½ cup coconut oil

½ cup applesauce

1 cup brown sugar

1 large egg

½ cup roasted, salted pumpkin seeds

½ cup dried cranberries

Line cookie sheet with parchment paper and set aside. Whisk together whole wheat flour, old-fashioned oats, baking soda, pumpkin pie spice, and salt. At medium speed, beat pumpkin, coconut oil, brown sugar, and egg until well combined; gradually beat in flour mixture, and then pumpkin seeds and cranberries. Scoop onto lined cookie sheet to form 16 mounds, spaced 2-inches apart. Flatten into disks. Bake at 350° F for 20 to 25 minutes or until dark brown on bottoms. Cool on wire rack. (Note: cooled cookies can be wrapped in plastic and stored at room temperature up to two days or frozen up to 2 weeks. Reheat in toaster until crisp.) Serves 16.

Nutritional Information: 175 calories; 8g fat (39.2% calories from fat); 3g protein; 25g carbohydrate; 3g dietary fiber; 13mg cholesterol; 122mg sodium.

Live It Tracker: 1 oz.-eq. grain.

DAY 7 | LUNCH

Creamy Tomato Soup

2 cups fat-free, less-sodium chicken broth

1 cup onion, chopped

¾ cup celery, chopped

1 tbsp. fresh basil, thinly sliced

1 tbsp. tomato paste

2 lbs. plum tomatoes, cut into wedges

½ tsp. salt

¼ tsp. freshly ground black pepper

6 tbps. plain lowfat yogurt

3 tbsp. fresh basil, thinly sliced

Combine first 6 ingredients in a large saucepan; bring to a boil. Reduce heat and simmer 30 minutes. Place half of tomato mixture in a blender. Remove center piece of blender lid (to allow steam to escape); secure blender lid on blender. Place a clean towel over opening in blender lid (to avoid splatters). Blend until smooth. Pour into a large bowl. Repeat procedure with remaining tomato mixture. Stir in salt and pepper. Ladle soup into each of 3 bowls; top each serving with 1 tablespoon yogurt and 1½ teaspoons basil. Serves 3.

Serve with: 10 crackers and piece of fruit (adds 1 oz.-eq grains and 1 cup fruit).

Nutritional Information: 170 calories; 2g fat (8.9% calories from fat); 12g protein; 22g carbohydrate; 4g dietary fiber; 2mg cholesterol; 403mg sodium.

Live It Tracker: 1 oz.-eq. protein; 1½ cups vegetables.

DAY 7 | DINNER

Lemon Steak with Zucchini

1½ lbs. flank steak, sliced into strips
4 medium zucchini
2 tbsp. olive oil
4 garlic cloves, minced
2 tbsp. butter
1 lemon, juice and zest
¼ cup low-sodium chicken broth
¼ cup parsley, chopped
¼ tsp. crushed red pepper flakes
salt and fresh cracked pepper, to taste

Marinade:
1/3 cup low-sodium soy sauce
¼ cup lemon juice
¼ cup olive oil
1 tbsp. hot chili sauce

Combine the ingredients for the marinade in a zip-lock bag. Add the steak strips, seal, and marinate in the refrigerator for 30 minutes to one hour. Wash and trim the ends of the zucchini. Using a spiralizer, make the zucchini noodles; set aside. Bring the steak to room temperature and heat oil in a large skillet over medium-high heat. Reserve the juices of the marinade for later. Add the steak and season with salt and pepper. Cook for one minute, and then add minced garlic. Stir the steak for another minute or two to cook the other side. Remove the steak from the skillet and set aside to a plate. In the same skillet, add butter, lemon juice and zest, red pepper flakes, chicken broth, and remaining marinade juices. Bring to a simmer and allow to reduce for 2 to 3 minutes, stirring regularly. Stir in the fresh parsley, and then add the zucchini noodles and toss for two to three minutes to cook. Add the steak strips back to the pan and stir for another minute. Serves 4.

Serve with: side salad with cherry tomatoes and cucumber and 4-inch slice of French bread (adds 1 oz.-eq. grains and ½ cup vegetables).

Nutritional Information: 485 calories; 38g fat (69.1% calories from fat); 27g protein; 12g carbohydrate; 3g dietary fiber; 73mg cholesterol; 949mg sodium.

Live It Tracker: 3½ oz.-eq. protein; 1½ cups vegetables.

STEPS FOR SPIRITUAL GROWTH

— GOD'S WORD FOR YOUR LIFE

I have hidden your word in my heart that I might not sin against you.
PSALM 119:11

As you begin to make decisions based on what God's Word teaches you, you will want to memorize what He has promised to those who trust and follow Him. Second Peter 1:3 tells us that God "has given us everything we need for life and godliness through *our knowledge of him*" (emphasis added). The Bible provides instruction and encouragement for any area of life in which you may be struggling. If you are dealing with a particular emotion or traumatic life event—fear, discouragement, stress, financial upset, the death of a loved one, a relationship difficulty—you can search through a Bible concordance for Scripture passages that deal with that particular situation. Scripture provides great comfort to those who memorize it.

One of the promises of knowing and obeying God's Word is that it gives you wisdom, insight, and understanding above all worldly knowledge (see Psalm 119:97–104). Psalm 119:129–130 says, "Your statutes are wonderful; therefore I obey them. The unfolding of your words gives light; it gives understanding to the simple." Now that's a precious promise about guidance for life!

The Value of Scripture Memory

Scripture memory is an important part of the Christian life. There are four key reasons to memorize Scripture:

1. **TO HANDLE DIFFICULT SITUATIONS.** A heartfelt knowledge of God's Word will equip you to handle any situation that you might face. Declaring such truth as, "I can do everything through Christ" (see Philippians 4:13) and "he will never leave me or forsake me" (see Hebrews 13:5) will enable you to walk through situations with peace and courage.

2. **TO OVERCOME TEMPTATION.** Luke 4:1–13 describes how Jesus used Scripture to overcome His temptations in the desert (see also

Matthew 4:1-11). Knowledge of Scripture and the strength that comes with the ability to use it are important parts of putting on the full armor of God in preparation for spiritual warfare (see Ephesians 6:10–18).

3. TO GET GUIDANCE. Psalm 119:105 states the Word of God "is a lamp to my feet and a light for my path." You learn to hide God's Word in your heart so His light will direct your decisions and actions throughout your day.

4. TO TRANSFORM YOUR MIND. "Do not conform any longer to the pattern of this world, but be transformed by the renewing of your mind" (Romans 12:2). Scripture memory allows you to replace a lie with the truth of God's Word. When Scripture becomes firmly settled in your memory, not only will your thoughts connect with God's thoughts, but you will also be able to honor God with small everyday decisions as well as big life-impacting ones. Scripture memorization is the key to making a permanent lifestyle change in your thought patterns, which brings balance to every other area of your life.

Scripture Memory Tips

- Write the verse down, saying it aloud as you write it.
- Read verses before and after the memory verse to get its context.
- Read the verse several times, emphasizing a different word each time.
- Connect the Scripture reference to the first few words.
- Locate patterns, phrases, or keywords.
- Apply the Scripture to circumstances you are now experiencing.
- Pray the verse, making it personal to your life and inserting your name as the recipient of the promise or teaching. (Try that with 1 Corinthians 10:13, inserting "me" and "I" for "you.")

- Review the verse every day until it becomes second nature to think those words whenever your circumstances match its message. The Holy Spirit will bring the verse to mind when you need it most if you decide to plant it in your memory.

- Use the First Place for Health memory aids, such as the memory verse cards found at the back of each Bible study, and the Scripture Memory CD found in a pocket on the inside back cover of each Bible study. (By using the CDs, you can exercise to music at the same time you are hiding God's Word in your heart.)

Scripture Memorization Made Easy!

What is your learning style? Do you learn by hearing, by sight, or by doing?

If you learn by hearing—if you are an auditory learner—singing the Scripture memory verses, reading them aloud, or recording them and listening to your recording will be very helpful in the memorization process.

If you are a visual learner, writing the verses and repeatedly reading through them will cement them in your mind.

If you learn by doing—if you are a tactile learner—creating motions for the words or using sign language will enable you to more easily recall the verse.

After determining your learning style, link your Scripture memory with a daily task, such as driving to work, walking on a treadmill, or eating lunch. Use these daily tasks as opportunities to memorize and review your verses.

Meals at home or out with friends can be used as a time to share the verse you are memorizing with those at your table. You could close your personal email messages by typing in your weekly memory verse. Or why not say your memory verse every time you brush your teeth or put on your shoes?

The purpose of Scripture memorization is to be able to apply God's words to your life. If you memorize Scripture using methods that connect with your particular learning style, you will find it easier to hide God's Word in your heart.

SPIRITUAL GROWTH

— ESTABLISHING A QUIET TIME

Like all other components of the First Place for Health program, developing a live relationship with God is not a random act. You must intentionally seek God if you are to find Him! It's not that God plays hide-and-seek with you. He is always available to you. He invites you to come boldly into His presence. He reveals Himself to you in the pages of the Bible. And once you decide to earnestly seek Him, you are sure to find Him! When you delight in Him, your gracious God will give you the desires of your heart. Spending time getting to know God involves four basic elements: a priority, a plan, a place, and practice.

A Priority

You can successfully establish a quiet time with God by making this meeting a daily priority. This may require carving out time in your day so you have time and space for this new relationship you are cultivating. Often this will mean eliminating less important things so you will have time and space to meet with God. When speaking about Jesus, John the Baptist said, "He must become greater; I must become less" (John 3:30). You will undoubtedly find that to be true as well. What might you need to eliminate from your current schedule so that spending quality time with God can become a priority?

A Plan

Having made quiet time a priority, you will want to come up with a plan. This plan will include the time you have set aside to spend with God and a general outline of how you will spend your time in God's presence. Elements you should consider incorporating into your quiet time include the following:

- Singing a song of praise

- Reading a daily selection in a devotional book or reading a psalm

- Using a systematic Scripture reading plan so you will be exposed to the whole truth of God's Word

- Completing your First Place for Health Bible study for that day

- Praying—silent, spoken, and written prayer

- Writing in your spiritual journal

You will also want to make a list of the materials you will need to make your encounter with God more meaningful:

- A Bible

- Your First Place for Health Bible study

- Your prayer journal

- A pen and/or pencil

- A devotional book

- A Bible concordance

- A college-level dictionary

- A tape or CD player, if music and praise songs will be part of your quiet time

- A box of tissues (tears—both of sadness and joy—are often part of our quiet time with God!)

SPIRITUAL GROWTH

Think of how you would plan an important business meeting or social event, and then transfer that knowledge to your meeting time with God.

A Place

Having formulated a meeting-with-God plan, you will next need to create a meeting-with-God place. Of course, God is always with you; however, in order to have quality devotional time with Him, it is desirable that you find a comfortable meeting place. You will want to select a spot that is quiet and as distraction-free as possible. Meeting with God in the same place on a regular basis will help you remember what you are there for: to have an encounter with the true and living God!

Having selected the place, put the materials you have determined to use in your quiet time into a basket or on a nearby table or shelf. Now take the time to establish your personal quiet time with God. Tailor your quiet time to fit your needs—and the time you have allotted to spend with God. Although many people elect to meet with God early in the morning, for others afternoon or evening is best. There is no hard-and-fast rule about when your quiet time should be—the only essential thing is that you establish a quiet time!

Start with a small amount of time that you know you can devote yourself to daily. You can be confident that as you consistently spend time with God each day, the amount of time you can spend will increase as you are ready for the next level of your walk with God.

I will meet with God from _____ to _____ daily.

I plan to use that time with God to _____ .

Supplies I will need to assemble include _____

_____ .

My meeting place with God will be _____

_____ .

Practice

After you have chosen the time and place to meet God each day and you have assembled your supplies, there are four easy steps for having a fruitful and worshipful time with the Lord.

STEP 1: Clear Your Heart and Mind

"Be still, and know that I am God" (Psalm 46:10). Begin your quiet time by reading the daily Bible selection from a devotional guide or a psalm. If you are new in your Christian walk, an excellent devotional guide to use is *Streams in the Desert* by L.B. Cowman. More mature Christians might benefit from *My Utmost for His Highest* by Oswald Chambers. Of course, you can use any devotional that has a strong emphasis on Scripture and prayer. (Note that we have included more choices in the "First Place for Health Recommended Resources" in the back of this member's guide.)

STEP 2: Read and Interact with Scripture

"I have hidden your word in my heart that I might not sin against you" (Psalm 119:11). As you open your Bible, ask the Holy Spirit to reveal something He knows you need for this day through the reading of His Word. Always try to find a nugget to encourage or direct you through the day. As you read the passage, pay special attention to the words and phrases the Holy Spirit brings to your attention. Some words may seem to resonate in your soul. You will want to spend time meditating on the passage, asking God what lesson He is teaching you. After reading the Scripture passage over several times, ask yourself the following questions:

- In light of what I have read today, is there something I must now do? (Confess a sin? Claim a promise? Follow an example? Obey a command? Avoid a situation?)

- *How should I respond to what I've read today?*

STEP 3: Pray

"Be clear minded and self-controlled so that you can pray" (1 Peter 4:7). Spend time conversing with the Lord in prayer. Prayer is such an important part of First Place for Health that there is an entire section in this member's guide devoted to the practice of prayer.

STEP 4: Praise

"Praise the LORD, O my soul, and forget not all his benefits" (Psalm 103:2). End your quiet time with a time of praise. Be sure to thank the Lord of heaven and warth for choosing to spend time with you!

— SHARING YOUR FAITH

Nothing is more effective in drawing someone to Jesus than sharing personal life experiences. People are more open to the good news of Jesus Christ when they see faith in action. Personal faith stories are simple and effective ways to share what Christ is doing in your life, because they show firsthand how Christ makes a difference.

Sharing your faith story has an added benefit: it builds you up in your faith, too! Is your experience in First Place for Health providing you opportunities to share with others what God is doing in your life? If you answered yes, then you have a personal faith story!

If you do not have a personal faith story, perhaps it is because you don't know Jesus Christ as your personal Lord and Savior. Read through "Steps to Becoming a Christian" (which is the next chapter) and begin today to give Christ first place in your life.

Creativity and preparation in using opportunities to share a word or story about Jesus is an important part of the Christian life. Is Jesus helping you in a special way? Are you achieving a level of success or peace that you haven't experienced in other attempts to lose weight, exercise regularly, or eat healthier? As people see you making changes and achieving success, they may ask you how you are doing it. How will—or do—you respond? Remember, your story is unique, and it may allow others to see what Christ is doing in your life. It may also help to bring Christ into the life of another person.

Personal Statements of Faith

First Place for Health gives you a great opportunity to communicate your faith and express what God is doing in your life. Be ready to use your own personal statement of faith whenever the opportunity presents itself. Personal statements of faith should be short and fit naturally into a conversation. They don't require or expect any action or response from the listener. The goal is not to get another person to change but simply to help you communicate who you are and what's important to you. Here are some examples of short statements of faith that you might use when someone asks what you are doing to lose weight:

- "I've been meeting with a group at my church. We pray together, support each other, learn about nutrition, and study the Bible."

- "It's amazing how Bible study and prayer are helping me lose weight and eat healthier."

- "I've had a lot of support from a group I meet with at church."

- "I'm relying more on God to help me make changes in my lifestyle."

Begin keeping a list of your meaningful experiences as you go through the First Place for Health program. Also notice what is happening in the lives of others. Use the following questions to help you prepare short personal statements and stories of faith:

- What is God doing in your life physically, mentally, emotionally, and spiritually?

- How has your relationship with God changed? Is it more intimate or personal?

- How are prayer, Bible study, and/or the support of others helping you achieve your goals for a healthy weight and good nutrition?

Writing Your Personal Faith Story

Write a brief story about how God is working in your life through First Place for Health. Use your story to help you share with others what's happening in your life. Use the following questions to help develop your story:

- Why did you join First Place for Health? What specific circumstances led you to a Christ-centered health and weight-loss program? What were you feeling when you joined?

- What was your relationship with Christ when you started First Place for Health? What is it now?

- Has your experience in First Place for Health changed your relationship with Christ? With yourself? With others?

- How has your relationship with Christ, prayer, Bible study, and group support made a difference in your life?

- What specific verse or passage of Scripture has made a difference in the way you view yourself or your relationship with Christ?

- What experiences have impacted your life since starting First Place for Health?

- In what ways is Christ working in your life today? In what ways is He meeting your needs?

- How has Christ worked in other members of your First Place for Health group?

Answer the above questions in a few sentences, and then use your answers to help you write your own short personal faith story.

ENDNOTES

WEEK ONE: THE POWER OF THE MIND

1. John Ortberg, *If You Want to Walk on Water, You've Got to Get Out of the Boat*, (Grand Rapids: Zondervan, 2001), 162.
2. Webster's New World Dictionary and Thesaurus, s.v. "conform" (New York: Houghton Mifflin, 2002).
3. Katie Barclay Wilkinson, "May the Mind of Christ, My Savior," written 1925.

WEEK TWO: WHAT'S GOD LIKE?

1. http://www.faithgateway.com/a-w-tozer-what-is-god-like/#.Wqm56WbMzYK
2. http://library.timelesstruths.org/music/The_Love_of_God/
3. https://bible.org/seriespage/5-holiness-god
4. David Jeremiah, My Heart's Desire: Living Every Moment in the Wonder of Worship, (Nashville: Thomas Nelson, 2004), 18.

WEEK THREE: PRAYER: CONVERSING WITH GOD

1. http://www.wow4u.com/qprayer4/
2. https://www.christianquotes.info/top-quotes/22-motivating-quotes-about-prayer/#axzz51w5Cdul1

WEEK FOUR: REFRAMING OBEDIENCE

1. A.W. Tozer, The Knowledge of the Holy (San Fransisco: Harper and Row Publishers, 1961), 66.
2. https://www.biblestudytools.com/commentaries/treasury-of-david/psalms-119-165.html
3. Nancy Leigh DeMoss, Surrender: The Heart God Controls (Chicago: Moody Publishers, 2003), 34-35.
4. https://bible.org/seriespage/lesson-78-true-humility-romans-123

WEEK FIVE: WHAT DOES GOD THINK ABOUT ME?

1. Grace Fox, Moving From Fear to Freedom: A Woman's Guide to Peace in Every Situation (Eugene: Harvest House Publishers, 2007)

WEEK SIX: MOVING FROM FEAR TO FREEDOM

1. Henry T. Blackaby and Claude V. King, Experiencing God Workbook (Nashville: LifeWay Press, 1990), 108.
2. Grace Fox, Moving From Fear to Freedom: A Woman's Guide to Peace in Every Situation (Eugene: Harvest House Publishers, 2007)
3. Rick Renner, Sparkling Gems (Tulsa: Harrison House Publishers, 2003), 325
4. https://www.forbes.com/sites/alicegwalton/2015/02/09/7-ways-meditation-can-actually-change-the-brain/#4fd9d3e31465

WEEK SEVEN: KEEPING FIRST THINGS FIRST

1. J.C. Ryle, Holiness (Toronto, Canada: The Institute of Evangelism, 1996) 28.
2. https://www.cnn.com/2016/06/30/health/americans-screen-time-nielsen/index.html
3. https://www.christianquotes.info/quotes-by-topic/quotes-about-time/#ixzz571pqyUC9
4. http://www.sermonindex.net/modules/newbb/viewtopic.php?topic_id=50607&forum=40
5. http://www.azquotes.com/quote/799020
6. https://www.goodreads.com/quotes/4439866-to-maintain-a-lifestyle-of-worship-we-must-attend-to

WEEK EIGHT: WHEN LIFE IS HARD

[1] https://www.preachingtoday.com/illustrations/2016/may/4050916.html
[2] https://www.brainpickings.org/2014/01/29/carol-dweck-mindset/
[3] Rick Renner, Sparking Gems (Tulsa: Harrison House Publishers, 2003), 147.

WEEK NINE: IT'S NOT ALL ABOUT ME

[1] https://www.christianquotes.info/quotes-by-topic/quotes-about-relationships/?listpage=3&instance=2#participants-list-2
[2] https://www.deseretnews.com/top/817/48/Friendship-Top-100-CS-Lewis-quotes-.html
[3] https://www.christianquotes.info/top-quotes/15-powerful-quotes-about-unity/#axzz596eopBzo
[4] Gari Meacham, Be Free, (Houston: First Place for Health, 2017), 51.

WEEK TEN: FORGIVENESS: WHAT IT IS, WHAT IT IS NOT

[1] Billy Graham, Nearing Home: Life, Faith, and Finishing Well (Nashville: Thomas Nelson, 2011), 125.

MEMBER SURVEY

Please answer the following questions to help your leader plan your First Place for Health meeting so that your needs might be met in this session. Give this form to your leader at the first group meeting.

Name _____ Birth date _____

Please list those who live in your household

Name   Relationship   Age

_____
_____
_____
_____

What church do you attend? _____

Would you like to receive more information   Yes   No
about our church?

Occupation _____

What talent or area of expertise would you be willing to share with our class?

_____
_____

Why did you join First Place for Health?

_____
_____

With notice, would you be willing to lead a Bible study   Yes   No
discussion one week?

Are you comfortable praying out loud? _____

If the assistant leader were absent, would you be willing   Yes   No
to assist weighing in memebers and possibly evaluating
the Live It Trackers?

Any other comments:

_____
_____

PERSONAL WEIGHT AND MEASUREMENT RECORD

WEEK	WEIGHT	+ OR -	GOAL THIS SESSION	POUNDS TO GOAL
1				
2				
3				
4				
5				
6				
7				
8				
9				
10				
11				
12				

BEGINNING MEASUREMENTS

WAIST _____ HIPS _____ THIGHS _____ CHEST _____

ENDING MEASUREMENTS

WAIST _____ HIPS _____ THIGHS _____ CHEST _____

PRAYER PARTNER WEEK 1
THE POWER OF THE MIND

*Love the Lord your God with all your
heart and with all your soul and with all your
mind and with all your strength.*

MARK 12:30

Date: _____

Name: _____

Home Phone: _____

Work Phone: _____

Email: _____

Personal Prayer Concerns:

_____
_____
_____
_____
_____
_____
_____
_____

This form is for prayer requests that are personal to you and your journey in First Place for Health. Please complete this form and have it ready to turn in when you arrive at your group meeting.

PRAYER PARTNER WEEK 2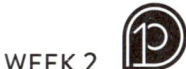
WHAT'S GOD LIKE?

No one is like you, O Lord; you are great, and your name is mighty in power. Who should not revere you, O King of the nations? This is your due.

JEREMIAH 10:6-7

Date: _____

Name: _____

Home Phone: _____

Work Phone: _____

Email: _____

Personal Prayer Concerns:

_____
_____
_____
_____
_____
_____
_____
_____

This form is for prayer requests that are personal to you and your journey in First Place for Health. Please complete this form and have it ready to turn in when you arrive at your group meeting.

PRAYER PARTNER WEEK 3

PRAYER: CONVERSING WITH GOD

Do not be anxious about anything, but in every situation, by prayer and petition, with thanksgiving, present your requests to God.

PHILIPPIANS 4:6

Date: _____

Name: _____

Home Phone: _____

Work Phone: _____

Email: _____

Personal Prayer Concerns:

_____
_____
_____
_____
_____
_____
_____
_____
_____

This form is for prayer requests that are personal to you and your journey in First Place for Health. Please complete this form and have it ready to turn in when you arrive at your group meeting.

PRAYER PARTNER
REFRAMING OBEDIENCE

WEEK 4

Observe what the Lord your God requires: Walk in obedience to him, and keep his decrees and commands, his laws and regulations, as written in the Law of Moses. Do this so that you may prosper in all you do and wherever you go. . .

1 KINGS 2:3

Date: _____

Name: _____

Home Phone: _____

Work Phone: _____

Email: _____

Personal Prayer Concerns:

_____

_____

_____

_____

_____

_____

_____

_____

_____

This form is for prayer requests that are personal to you and your journey in First Place for Health. Please complete this form and have it ready to turn in when you arrive at your group meeting.

PRAYER PARTNER   WEEK 5

WHAT DOES GOD THINK ABOUT ME?

How precious to me are your thoughts, God! How vast is the sum of them! Were I to count them, they would outnumber the grains of sand—when I awake, I am still with you.

PSALM 139:17-18

Date: _____

Name: _____

Home Phone: _____

Work Phone: _____

Email: _____

Personal Prayer Concerns:

_____
_____
_____
_____
_____
_____
_____
_____
_____

This form is for prayer requests that are personal to you and your journey in First Place for Health. Please complete this form and have it ready to turn in when you arrive at your group meeting.

PRAYER PARTNER  WEEK 6

MOVING FROM FEAR TO FREEDOM

*I sought the Lord, and he answered me; he delivered
me from all my fears. Those who look to him are
radiant; their faces are never covered with shame.*

PSALM 34:4-5

Date: _____

Name: _____

Home Phone: _____

Work Phone: _____

Email: _____

Personal Prayer Concerns:

_____
_____
_____
_____
_____
_____
_____
_____

This form is for prayer requests that are personal to you and your journey in First Place for Health. Please complete this form and have it ready to turn in when you arrive at your group meeting.

PRAYER PARTNER WEEK 7

KEEPING FIRST THINGS FIRST

But seek first his kingdom and his righteousness,
and all these things will be given to you as well.

MATTHEW 6:33

Date: _____

Name: _____

Home Phone: _____

Work Phone: _____

Email: _____

Personal Prayer Concerns:

_____

_____

_____

_____

_____

_____

_____

_____

This form is for prayer requests that are personal to you and your journey in First Place for Health. Please complete this form and have it ready to turn in when you arrive at your group meeting.

PRAYER PARTNER WEEK 8

WHEN LIFE IS HARD

I have told you these things, so that in me you may have peace. In this world you will have trouble. But take heart! I have overcome the world.

JOHN 16:33

Date: _____

Name: _____

Home Phone: _____

Work Phone: _____

Email: _____

Personal Prayer Concerns:

_____
_____
_____
_____
_____
_____
_____
_____

This form is for prayer requests that are personal to you and your journey in First Place for Health. Please complete this form and have it ready to turn in when you arrive at your group meeting.

PRAYER PARTNER WEEK 9
IT'S NOT ALL ABOUT ME

Do nothing out of selfish ambition or vain conceit. Rather, in humility value others above yourselves, not looking to your own interests but each of you to the interests of the others.

PHILIPPIANS 2:3-4

Date: _____

Name: _____

Home Phone: _____

Work Phone: _____

Email: _____

Personal Prayer Concerns:

_____
_____
_____
_____
_____
_____
_____
_____
_____

This form is for prayer requests that are personal to you and your journey in First Place for Health. Please complete this form and have it ready to turn in when you arrive at your group meeting.

PRAYER PARTNER WEEK 10

FORGIVENESS: WHAT IT IS, WHAT IT IS NOT

And forgive us our debts, as we also have forgiven our debtors.

MATTHEW 6:12

Date: _____

Name: _____

Home Phone: _____

Work Phone: _____

Email: _____

Personal Prayer Concerns:

_____

_____

_____

_____

_____

_____

_____

_____

This form is for prayer requests that are personal to you and your journey in First Place for Health. Please complete this form and have it ready to turn in when you arrive at your group meeting.

100-MILE CLUB

WALKING			
slowly, 2 mph	30 min =	156 cal =	1 mile
moderately, 3 mph	20 min =	156 cal =	1 mile
very briskly, 4 mph	15 min =	156 cal =	1 mile
speed walking	10 min =	156 cal =	1 mile
up stairs	13 min =	159 cal =	1 mile
RUNNING / JOGGING			
. . .	10 min =	156 cal =	1 mile
CYCLE OUTDOORS			
slowly, < 10 mph	20 min =	156 cal =	1 mile
light effort, 10-12 mph	12 min =	156 cal =	1 mile
moderate effort, 12-14 mph	10 min =	156 cal =	1 mile
vigorous effort, 14-16 mph	7.5 min =	156 cal =	1 mile
very fast, 16-19 mph	6.5 min =	152 cal =	1 mile
SPORTS ACTIVITIES			
playing tennis (singles)	10 min =	156 cal =	1 mile
swimming			
light to moderate effort	11 min =	152 cal =	1 mile
fast, vigorous effort	7.5 min =	156 cal =	1 mile
softball	15 min =	156 cal =	1 mile
golf	20 min =	156 cal =	1 mile
rollerblading	6.5 min =	152 cal =	1 mile
ice skating	11 min =	152 cal =	1 mile
jumping rope	7.5 min =	156 cal =	1 mile
basketball	12 min =	156 cal =	1 mile
soccer (casual)	15 min =	159 min =	1 mile
AROUND THE HOUSE			
mowing grass	22 min =	156 cal =	1 mile
mopping, sweeping, vacuuming	19.5 min =	155 cal =	1 mile
cooking	40 min =	160 cal =	1 mile
gardening	19 min =	156 cal =	1 mile
housework (general)	35 min =	156 cal =	1 mile

AROUND THE HOUSE			
ironing	45 min =	153 cal =	1 mile
raking leaves	25 min =	150 cal =	1 mile
washing car	23 min =	156 cal =	1 mile
washing dishes	45 min =	153 cal =	1 mile
AT THE GYM			
stair machine	8.5 min =	155 cal =	1 mile
stationary bike			
slowly, 10 mph	30 min =	156 cal =	1 mile
moderately, 10-13 mph	15 min =	156 cal =	1 mile
vigorously, 13-16 mph	7.5 min =	156 cal =	1 mile
briskly, 16-19 mph	6.5 min =	156 cal =	1 mile
elliptical trainer	12 min =	156 cal =	1 mile
weight machines (vigorously)	13 min =	152 cal =	1 mile
aerobics			
low impact	15 min =	156 cal =	1 mile
high impact	12 min =	156 cal =	1 mile
water	20 min =	156 cal =	1 mile
pilates	15 min =	156 cal =	1 mile
raquetball (casual)	15 min =	156 cal =	1 mile
stretching exercises	25 min =	150 cal =	1 mile
weight lifting (also works for weight machines used moderately or gently)	30 min =	156 cal =	1 mile
FAMILY LEISURE			
playing piano	37 min =	155 cal =	1 mile
jumping rope	10 min =	152 cal =	1 mile
skating (moderate)	20 min =	152 cal =	1 mile
swimming			
moderate	17 min =	156 cal =	1 mile
vigorous	10 min =	148 cal =	1 mile
table tennis	25 min =	150 cal =	1 mile
walk / run / play with kids	25 min =	150 cal =	1 mile

LIVE IT TRACKER

Name: _____

My activity goal for next week:
○ None ○ <30 min/day ○ 30-60 min/day

My food goal for next week: _____
_____

Date: _____ Week #: _____

loss/gain _____ Calorie Range: _____

My week at a glace:
○ Great ○ So-so ○ Not so great

Activity level:
○ None ○ <30 min/day ○ 30-60 min/day

RECOMMENDED DAILY AMOUNT OF FOOD FROM EACH GROUP

GROUP	DAILY CALORIES							
	1300-1400	1500-1600	1700-1800	1900-2000	2100-2200	2300-2400	2500-2600	2700-2800
Fruits	1.5 – 2 c.	1.5 – 2 c.	1.5 – 2 c.	2 – 2.5 c.	2 – 2.5 c.	2.5 – 3.5 c.	3.5 – 4.5 c.	3.5 – 4.5 c.
Vegetables	1.5 – 2 c.	2 – 2.5 c.	2.5 – 3 c.	2.5 – 3 c.	3 – 3.5 c.	3.5 – 4.5 c.	4.5 – 5 c.	4.5 – 5 c.
Grains	5 oz eq.	5-6 oz eq.	6-7 oz eq.	6-7 oz eq.	7-8 oz eq.	8-9 oz eq.	9-10 oz eq.	10-11 oz eq.
Dairy	2-3 c.	3 c.	3 c.	3 c.	3 c.	3 c.	3 c.	3 c.
Protein	4 oz eq.	5 oz eq.	5-5.5 oz eq.	5.5-6.5 oz eq.	6.5-7 oz eq.	7-7.5 oz eq.	7-7.5 oz eq.	7.5-8 oz eq.
Healthy Oils & Other Fats	4 tsp.	5 tsp.	5 tsp.	6 tsp.	6 tsp.	7 tsp.	8 tsp.	8 tsp.
Water & Super Beverages*	Women: 9 c. Men: 13 c.	Women: 9 c. Men: 13 c.	Women: 9 c. Men: 13 c.	Women: 9 c. Men: 13 c.	Women: 9 c. Men: 13 c.	Women: 9 c. Men: 13 c.	Women: 9 c. Men: 13 c.	Women: 9 c. Men: 13 c.

*May count up to 3 cups caffeinated tea or coffee toward goal

DAILY FOOD GROUP TRACKER

GROUP	FRUITS	VEGETABLES	GRAINS	PROTEIN	DAIRY	HEALTHY OILS & OTHER FATS	WATER & SUPER BEVERAGES
❶ Estimate Total							
❷ Estimate Total							
❸ Estimate Total							
❹ Estimate Total							
❺ Estimate Total							
❻ Estimate Total							
❼ Estimate Total							

FOOD CHOICES **DAY ❶**

Breakfast: _____
Lunch: _____
Dinner: _____
Snacks: _____

PHYSICAL ACTIVITY steps/miles/minutes: _____

description: _____

SPIRITUAL ACTIVITY

description: _____

FOOD CHOICES — **DAY ❷**
Breakfast: _____
Lunch: _____
Dinner: _____
Snacks: _____

PHYSICAL ACTIVITY   steps/miles/minutes: _____ | **SPIRITUAL ACTIVITY**
description: _____ | description: _____

FOOD CHOICES — **DAY ❸**
Breakfast: _____
Lunch: _____
Dinner: _____
Snacks: _____

PHYSICAL ACTIVITY   steps/miles/minutes: _____ | **SPIRITUAL ACTIVITY**
description: _____ | description: _____

FOOD CHOICES — **DAY ❹**
Breakfast: _____
Lunch: _____
Dinner: _____
Snacks: _____

PHYSICAL ACTIVITY   steps/miles/minutes: _____ | **SPIRITUAL ACTIVITY**
description: _____ | description: _____

FOOD CHOICES — **DAY ❺**
Breakfast: _____
Lunch: _____
Dinner: _____
Snacks: _____

PHYSICAL ACTIVITY   steps/miles/minutes: _____ | **SPIRITUAL ACTIVITY**
description: _____ | description: _____

FOOD CHOICES — **DAY ❻**
Breakfast: _____
Lunch: _____
Dinner: _____
Snacks: _____

PHYSICAL ACTIVITY   steps/miles/minutes: _____ | **SPIRITUAL ACTIVITY**
description: _____ | description: _____

FOOD CHOICES — **DAY ❼**
Breakfast: _____
Lunch: _____
Dinner: _____
Snacks: _____

PHYSICAL ACTIVITY   steps/miles/minutes: _____ | **SPIRITUAL ACTIVITY**
description: _____ | description: _____

LIVE IT TRACKER

Name: _____   Date: _____ Week #: _____

My activity goal for next week:
○ None   ○ <30 min/day   ○ 30-60 min/day

loss/gain _____ Calorie Range: _____

My week at a glace:
○ Great   ○ So-so   ○ Not so great

My food goal for next week: _____
_____

Activity level:
○ None   ○ <30 min/day   ○ 30-60 min/day

RECOMMENDED DAILY AMOUNT OF FOOD FROM EACH GROUP

GROUP	DAILY CALORIES							
	1300-1400	1500-1600	1700-1800	1900-2000	2100-2200	2300-2400	2500-2600	2700-2800
Fruits	1.5 – 2 c.	1.5 – 2 c.	1.5 – 2 c.	2 – 2.5 c.	2 – 2.5 c.	2.5 – 3.5 c.	3.5 – 4.5 c.	3.5 – 4.5 c.
Vegetables	1.5 – 2 c.	2 – 2.5 c.	2.5 – 3 c.	2.5 – 3 c.	3 – 3.5 c.	3.5 – 4.5 c.	4.5 – 5 c.	4.5 – 5 c.
Grains	5 oz eq.	5-6 oz eq.	6-7 oz eq.	6-7 oz eq.	7-8 oz eq.	8-9 oz eq.	9-10 oz eq.	10-11 oz eq.
Dairy	2-3 c.	3 c.	3 c.	3 c.	3 c.	3 c.	3 c.	3 c.
Protein	4 oz eq.	5 oz eq.	5-5.5 oz eq.	5.5-6.5 oz eq.	6.5-7 oz eq.	7-7.5 oz eq.	7-7.5 oz eq.	7.5-8 oz eq.
Healthy Oils & Other Fats	4 tsp.	5 tsp.	5 tsp.	6 tsp.	6 tsp.	7 tsp.	8 tsp.	8 tsp.
Water & Super Beverages*	Women: 9 c. Men: 13 c.	Women: 9 c. Men: 13 c.	Women: 9 c. Men: 13 c.	Women: 9 c. Men: 13 c.	Women: 9 c. Men: 13 c.	Women: 9 c. Men: 13 c.	Women: 9 c. Men: 13 c.	Women: 9 c. Men: 13 c.

*May count up to 3 cups caffeinated tea or coffee toward goal

DAILY FOOD GROUP TRACKER

GROUP	FRUITS	VEGETABLES	GRAINS	PROTEIN	DAIRY	HEALTHY OILS & OTHER FATS	WATER & SUPER BEVERAGES
❶ Estimate Total							
❷ Estimate Total							
❸ Estimate Total							
❹ Estimate Total							
❺ Estimate Total							
❻ Estimate Total							
❼ Estimate Total							

FOOD CHOICES   DAY ❶

Breakfast: _____
Lunch: _____
Dinner: _____
Snacks: _____

PHYSICAL ACTIVITY   steps/miles/minutes: _____   SPIRITUAL ACTIVITY

description: _____   description: _____

FOOD CHOICES — DAY 2
Breakfast: _____
Lunch: _____
Dinner: _____
Snacks: _____

PHYSICAL ACTIVITY steps/miles/minutes: _____ | **SPIRITUAL ACTIVITY**
description: _____ | description: _____

FOOD CHOICES — DAY 3
Breakfast: _____
Lunch: _____
Dinner: _____
Snacks: _____

PHYSICAL ACTIVITY steps/miles/minutes: _____ | **SPIRITUAL ACTIVITY**
description: _____ | description: _____

FOOD CHOICES — DAY 4
Breakfast: _____
Lunch: _____
Dinner: _____
Snacks: _____

PHYSICAL ACTIVITY steps/miles/minutes: _____ | **SPIRITUAL ACTIVITY**
description: _____ | description: _____

FOOD CHOICES — DAY 5
Breakfast: _____
Lunch: _____
Dinner: _____
Snacks: _____

PHYSICAL ACTIVITY steps/miles/minutes: _____ | **SPIRITUAL ACTIVITY**
description: _____ | description: _____

FOOD CHOICES — DAY 6
Breakfast: _____
Lunch: _____
Dinner: _____
Snacks: _____

PHYSICAL ACTIVITY steps/miles/minutes: _____ | **SPIRITUAL ACTIVITY**
description: _____ | description: _____

FOOD CHOICES — DAY 7
Breakfast: _____
Lunch: _____
Dinner: _____
Snacks: _____

PHYSICAL ACTIVITY steps/miles/minutes: _____ | **SPIRITUAL ACTIVITY**
description: _____ | description: _____

LIVE IT TRACKER

Name: _____

My activity goal for next week:
○ None ○ <30 min/day ○ 30-60 min/day

My food goal for next week: _____
_____

Date: _____ Week #: _____

loss /gain _____ Calorie Range: _____

My week at a glace:
○ Great ○ So-so ○ Not so great

Activity level:
○ None ○ <30 min/day ○ 30-60 min/day

RECOMMENDED DAILY AMOUNT OF FOOD FROM EACH GROUP

GROUP	DAILY CALORIES							
	1300-1400	1500-1600	1700-1800	1900-2000	2100-2200	2300-2400	2500-2600	2700-2800
Fruits	1.5 – 2 c.	1.5 – 2 c.	1.5 – 2 c.	2 – 2.5 c.	2 – 2.5 c.	2.5 – 3.5 c.	3.5 – 4.5 c.	3.5 – 4.5 c.
Vegetables	1.5 – 2 c.	2 – 2.5 c.	2.5 – 3 c.	2.5 – 3 c.	3 – 3.5 c.	3.5 – 4.5 c..	4.5 – 5 c.	4.5 – 5 c.
Grains	5 oz eq.	5-6 oz eq.	6-7 oz eq.	6-7 oz eq.	7-8 oz eq.	8-9 oz eq.	9-10 oz eq.	10-11 oz eq.
Dairy	2-3 c.	3 c.	3 c.	3 c.	3 c.	3 c.	3 c.	3 c.
Protein	4 oz eq.	5 oz eq.	5-5.5 oz eq.	5.5-6.5 oz eq.	6.5-7 oz eq.	7-7.5 oz eq.	7-7.5 oz eq.	7.5-8 oz eq.
Healthy Oils & Other Fats	4 tsp.	5 tsp.	5 tsp.	6 tsp.	6 tsp.	7 tsp.	8 tsp.	8 tsp.
Water & Super Beverages*	Women: 9 c. Men: 13 c.	Women: 9 c. Men: 13 c.	Women: 9 c. Men: 13 c.	Women: 9 c. Men: 13 c.	Women: 9 c. Men: 13 c.	Women: 9 c. Men: 13 c.	Women: 9 c. Men: 13 c.	Women: 9 c. Men: 13 c.

*May count up to 3 cups caffeinated tea or coffee toward goal

DAILY FOOD GROUP TRACKER

GROUP	FRUITS	VEGETABLES	GRAINS	PROTEIN	DAIRY	HEALTHY OILS & OTHER FATS	WATER & SUPER BEVERAGES
❶ Estimate Total							
❷ Estimate Total							
❸ Estimate Total							
❹ Estimate Total							
❺ Estimate Total							
❻ Estimate Total							
❼ Estimate Total							

FOOD CHOICES **DAY ❶**

Breakfast: _____
Lunch: _____
Dinner: _____
Snacks: _____

PHYSICAL ACTIVITY steps/miles/minutes: _____
description: _____

SPIRITUAL ACTIVITY
description: _____

FOOD CHOICES — DAY 2
Breakfast: _____
Lunch: _____
Dinner: _____
Snacks: _____

PHYSICAL ACTIVITY steps/miles/minutes: _____ **SPIRITUAL ACTIVITY**
description: _____ description: _____

FOOD CHOICES — DAY 3
Breakfast: _____
Lunch: _____
Dinner: _____
Snacks: _____

PHYSICAL ACTIVITY steps/miles/minutes: _____ **SPIRITUAL ACTIVITY**
description: _____ description: _____

FOOD CHOICES — DAY 4
Breakfast: _____
Lunch: _____
Dinner: _____
Snacks: _____

PHYSICAL ACTIVITY steps/miles/minutes: _____ **SPIRITUAL ACTIVITY**
description: _____ description: _____

FOOD CHOICES — DAY 5
Breakfast: _____
Lunch: _____
Dinner: _____
Snacks: _____

PHYSICAL ACTIVITY steps/miles/minutes: _____ **SPIRITUAL ACTIVITY**
description: _____ description: _____

FOOD CHOICES — DAY 6
Breakfast: _____
Lunch: _____
Dinner: _____
Snacks: _____

PHYSICAL ACTIVITY steps/miles/minutes: _____ **SPIRITUAL ACTIVITY**
description: _____ description: _____

FOOD CHOICES — DAY 7
Breakfast: _____
Lunch: _____
Dinner: _____
Snacks: _____

PHYSICAL ACTIVITY steps/miles/minutes: _____ **SPIRITUAL ACTIVITY**
description: _____ description: _____

LIVE IT TRACKER

Name: _____ Date: _____ Week #: _____

My activity goal for next week:
○ None   ○ <30 min/day   ○ 30-60 min/day

loss/gain _____ Calorie Range: _____

My week at a glance:
○ Great   ○ So-so   ○ Not so great

My food goal for next week: _____
_____

Activity level:
○ None   ○ <30 min/day   ○ 30-60 min/day

RECOMMENDED DAILY AMOUNT OF FOOD FROM EACH GROUP

GROUP	DAILY CALORIES							
	1300-1400	1500-1600	1700-1800	1900-2000	2100-2200	2300-2400	2500-2600	2700-2800
Fruits	1.5 – 2 c.	1.5 – 2 c.	1.5 – 2 c.	2 – 2.5 c.	2 – 2.5 c.	2.5 – 3.5 c.	3.5 – 4.5 c.	3.5 – 4.5 c.
Vegetables	1.5 – 2 c.	2 – 2.5 c.	2.5 – 3 c.	2.5 – 3 c.	3 – 3.5 c.	3.5 – 4.5 c.	4.5 – 5 c.	4.5 – 5 c.
Grains	5 oz eq.	5-6 oz eq.	6-7 oz eq.	6-7 oz eq.	7-8 oz eq.	8-9 oz eq.	9-10 oz eq.	10-11 oz eq.
Dairy	2-3 c.	3 c.	3 c.	3 c.	3 c.	3 c.	3 c.	3 c.
Protein	4 oz eq.	5 oz eq.	5-5.5 oz eq.	5.5-6.5 oz eq.	6.5-7 oz eq.	7-7.5 oz eq.	7-7.5 oz eq.	7.5-8 oz eq.
Healthy Oils & Other Fats	4 tsp.	5 tsp.	5 tsp.	6 tsp.	6 tsp.	7 tsp.	8 tsp.	8 tsp.
Water & Super Beverages*	Women: 9 c. Men: 13 c.	Women: 9 c. Men: 13 c.	Women: 9 c. Men: 13 c.	Women: 9 c. Men: 13 c.	Women: 9 c. Men: 13 c.	Women: 9 c. Men: 13 c.	Women: 9 c. Men: 13 c.	Women: 9 c. Men: 13 c.

*May count up to 3 cups caffeinated tea or coffee toward goal

DAILY FOOD GROUP TRACKER

GROUP	FRUITS	VEGETABLES	GRAINS	PROTEIN	DAIRY	HEALTHY OILS & OTHER FATS	WATER & SUPER BEVERAGES
❶ Estimate Total							
❷ Estimate Total							
❸ Estimate Total							
❹ Estimate Total							
❺ Estimate Total							
❻ Estimate Total							
❼ Estimate Total							

FOOD CHOICES   **DAY ❶**

Breakfast: _____
Lunch: _____
Dinner: _____
Snacks: _____

PHYSICAL ACTIVITY   steps/miles/minutes: _____
description: _____

SPIRITUAL ACTIVITY
description: _____

FOOD CHOICES — DAY 2
Breakfast: _____
Lunch: _____
Dinner: _____
Snacks: _____

PHYSICAL ACTIVITY steps/miles/minutes: _____ | **SPIRITUAL ACTIVITY**
description: _____ | description: _____

FOOD CHOICES — DAY 3
Breakfast: _____
Lunch: _____
Dinner: _____
Snacks: _____

PHYSICAL ACTIVITY steps/miles/minutes: _____ | **SPIRITUAL ACTIVITY**
description: _____ | description: _____

FOOD CHOICES — DAY 4
Breakfast: _____
Lunch: _____
Dinner: _____
Snacks: _____

PHYSICAL ACTIVITY steps/miles/minutes: _____ | **SPIRITUAL ACTIVITY**
description: _____ | description: _____

FOOD CHOICES — DAY 5
Breakfast: _____
Lunch: _____
Dinner: _____
Snacks: _____

PHYSICAL ACTIVITY steps/miles/minutes: _____ | **SPIRITUAL ACTIVITY**
description: _____ | description: _____

FOOD CHOICES — DAY 6
Breakfast: _____
Lunch: _____
Dinner: _____
Snacks: _____

PHYSICAL ACTIVITY steps/miles/minutes: _____ | **SPIRITUAL ACTIVITY**
description: _____ | description: _____

FOOD CHOICES — DAY 7
Breakfast: _____
Lunch: _____
Dinner: _____
Snacks: _____

PHYSICAL ACTIVITY steps/miles/minutes: _____ | **SPIRITUAL ACTIVITY**
description: _____ | description: _____

LIVE IT TRACKER

Name: _____

Date: _____ Week #: _____

My activity goal for next week:
- ○ None ○ <30 min/day ○ 30-60 min/day

loss /gain _____ Calorie Range: _____

My week at a glace:
- ○ Great ○ So-so ○ Not so great

My food goal for next week: _____
_____

Activity level:
- ○ None ○ <30 min/day ○ 30-60 min/day

RECOMMENDED DAILY AMOUNT OF FOOD FROM EACH GROUP

GROUP	DAILY CALORIES							
	1300-1400	1500-1600	1700-1800	1900-2000	2100-2200	2300-2400	2500-2600	2700-2800
Fruits	1.5 – 2 c.	1.5 – 2 c.	1.5 – 2 c.	2 – 2.5 c.	2 – 2.5 c.	2.5 – 3.5 c.	3.5 – 4.5 c.	3.5 – 4.5 c.
Vegetables	1.5 – 2 c.	2 – 2.5 c.	2.5 – 3 c.	2.5 – 3 c.	3 – 3.5 c.	3.5 – 4.5 c.	4.5 – 5 c.	4.5 – 5 c.
Grains	5 oz eq.	5-6 oz eq.	6-7 oz eq.	6-7 oz eq.	7-8 oz eq.	8-9 oz eq.	9-10 oz eq.	10-11 oz eq.
Dairy	2-3 c.	3 c.	3 c.	3 c.	3 c.	3 c.	3 c.	3 c.
Protein	4 oz eq.	5 oz eq.	5-5.5 oz eq.	5.5-6.5 oz eq.	6.5-7 oz eq.	7-7.5 oz eq.	7-7.5 oz eq.	7.5-8 oz eq.
Healthy Oils & Other Fats	4 tsp.	5 tsp.	5 tsp.	6 tsp.	6 tsp.	7 tsp.	8 tsp.	8 tsp.
Water & Super Beverages*	Women: 9 c. Men: 13 c.	Women: 9 c. Men: 13 c.	Women: 9 c. Men: 13 c.	Women: 9 c. Men: 13 c.	Women: 9 c. Men: 13 c.	Women: 9 c. Men: 13 c.	Women: 9 c. Men: 13 c.	Women: 9 c. Men: 13 c.

*May count up to 3 cups caffeinated tea or coffee toward goal

DAILY FOOD GROUP TRACKER

GROUP	FRUITS	VEGETABLES	GRAINS	PROTEIN	DAIRY	HEALTHY OILS & OTHER FATS	WATER & SUPER BEVERAGES
1 Estimate Total							
2 Estimate Total							
3 Estimate Total							
4 Estimate Total							
5 Estimate Total							
6 Estimate Total							
7 Estimate Total							

FOOD CHOICES   DAY 1

Breakfast: _____
Lunch: _____
Dinner: _____
Snacks: _____

PHYSICAL ACTIVITY   steps/miles/minutes: _____

description: _____

SPIRITUAL ACTIVITY

description: _____

FOOD CHOICES — DAY ❷
Breakfast: _____
Lunch: _____
Dinner: _____
Snacks: _____

PHYSICAL ACTIVITY steps/miles/minutes: _____
description: _____

SPIRITUAL ACTIVITY
description: _____

FOOD CHOICES — DAY ❸
Breakfast: _____
Lunch: _____
Dinner: _____
Snacks: _____

PHYSICAL ACTIVITY steps/miles/minutes: _____
description: _____

SPIRITUAL ACTIVITY
description: _____

FOOD CHOICES — DAY ❹
Breakfast: _____
Lunch: _____
Dinner: _____
Snacks: _____

PHYSICAL ACTIVITY steps/miles/minutes: _____
description: _____

SPIRITUAL ACTIVITY
description: _____

FOOD CHOICES — DAY ❺
Breakfast: _____
Lunch: _____
Dinner: _____
Snacks: _____

PHYSICAL ACTIVITY steps/miles/minutes: _____
description: _____

SPIRITUAL ACTIVITY
description: _____

FOOD CHOICES — DAY ❻
Breakfast: _____
Lunch: _____
Dinner: _____
Snacks: _____

PHYSICAL ACTIVITY steps/miles/minutes: _____
description: _____

SPIRITUAL ACTIVITY
description: _____

FOOD CHOICES — DAY ❼
Breakfast: _____
Lunch: _____
Dinner: _____
Snacks: _____

PHYSICAL ACTIVITY steps/miles/minutes: _____
description: _____

SPIRITUAL ACTIVITY
description: _____

LIVE IT TRACKER

Name: _____

Date: _____ Week #: _____

My activity goal for next week:
○ None ○ <30 min/day ○ 30-60 min/day

loss/gain _____ Calorie Range: _____

My week at a glance:
○ Great ○ So-so ○ Not so great

My food goal for next week: _____
_____

Activity level:
○ None ○ <30 min/day ○ 30-60 min/day

RECOMMENDED DAILY AMOUNT OF FOOD FROM EACH GROUP

GROUP	DAILY CALORIES							
	1300-1400	1500-1600	1700-1800	1900-2000	2100-2200	2300-2400	2500-2600	2700-2800
Fruits	1.5 – 2 c.	1.5 – 2 c.	1.5 – 2 c.	2 – 2.5 c.	2 – 2.5 c.	2.5 – 3.5 c.	3.5 – 4.5 c.	3.5 – 4.5 c.
Vegetables	1.5 – 2 c.	2 – 2.5 c.	2.5 – 3 c.	2.5 – 3 c.	3 – 3.5 c.	3.5 – 4.5 c.	4.5 – 5 c.	4.5 – 5 c.
Grains	5 oz eq.	5-6 oz eq.	6-7 oz eq.	6-7 oz eq.	7-8 oz eq.	8-9 oz eq.	9-10 oz eq.	10-11 oz eq.
Dairy	2-3 c.	3 c.	3 c.	3 c.	3 c.	3 c.	3 c.	3 c.
Protein	4 oz eq.	5 oz eq.	5-5.5 oz eq.	5.5-6.5 oz eq.	6.5-7 oz eq.	7-7.5 oz eq.	7-7.5 oz eq.	7.5-8 oz eq.
Healthy Oils & Other Fats	4 tsp.	5 tsp.	5 tsp.	6 tsp.	6 tsp.	7 tsp.	8 tsp.	8 tsp.
Water & Super Beverages*	Women: 9 c. Men: 13 c.	Women: 9 c. Men: 13 c.	Women: 9 c. Men: 13 c.	Women: 9 c. Men: 13 c.	Women: 9 c. Men: 13 c.	Women: 9 c. Men: 13 c.	Women: 9 c. Men: 13 c.	Women: 9 c. Men: 13 c.

*May count up to 3 cups caffeinated tea or coffee toward goal

DAILY FOOD GROUP TRACKER

GROUP	FRUITS	VEGETABLES	GRAINS	PROTEIN	DAIRY	HEALTHY OILS & OTHER FATS	WATER & SUPER BEVERAGES
1 Estimate Total							
2 Estimate Total							
3 Estimate Total							
4 Estimate Total							
5 Estimate Total							
6 Estimate Total							
7 Estimate Total							

FOOD CHOICES   DAY 1

Breakfast: _____
Lunch: _____
Dinner: _____
Snacks: _____

PHYSICAL ACTIVITY   steps/miles/minutes: _____

description: _____

SPIRITUAL ACTIVITY

description: _____

FOOD CHOICES — DAY 2
Breakfast: _____
Lunch: _____
Dinner: _____
Snacks: _____

PHYSICAL ACTIVITY steps/miles/minutes: _____ **SPIRITUAL ACTIVITY**
description: _____ description: _____

FOOD CHOICES — DAY 3
Breakfast: _____
Lunch: _____
Dinner: _____
Snacks: _____

PHYSICAL ACTIVITY steps/miles/minutes: _____ **SPIRITUAL ACTIVITY**
description: _____ description: _____

FOOD CHOICES — DAY 4
Breakfast: _____
Lunch: _____
Dinner: _____
Snacks: _____

PHYSICAL ACTIVITY steps/miles/minutes: _____ **SPIRITUAL ACTIVITY**
description: _____ description: _____

FOOD CHOICES — DAY 5
Breakfast: _____
Lunch: _____
Dinner: _____
Snacks: _____

PHYSICAL ACTIVITY steps/miles/minutes: _____ **SPIRITUAL ACTIVITY**
description: _____ description: _____

FOOD CHOICES — DAY 6
Breakfast: _____
Lunch: _____
Dinner: _____
Snacks: _____

PHYSICAL ACTIVITY steps/miles/minutes: _____ **SPIRITUAL ACTIVITY**
description: _____ description: _____

FOOD CHOICES — DAY 7
Breakfast: _____
Lunch: _____
Dinner: _____
Snacks: _____

PHYSICAL ACTIVITY steps/miles/minutes: _____ **SPIRITUAL ACTIVITY**
description: _____ description: _____

LIVE IT TRACKER

Name: _____

Date: _____ Week #: _____

My activity goal for next week:
○ None ○ <30 min/day ○ 30-60 min/day

loss /gain _____ Calorie Range: _____

My week at a glace:
○ Great ○ So-so ○ Not so great

My food goal for next week: _____
_____

Activity level:
○ None ○ <30 min/day ○ 30-60 min/day

RECOMMENDED DAILY AMOUNT OF FOOD FROM EACH GROUP

GROUP	DAILY CALORIES							
	1300-1400	1500-1600	1700-1800	1900-2000	2100-2200	2300-2400	2500-2600	2700-2800
Fruits	1.5 – 2 c.	1.5 – 2 c.	1.5 – 2 c.	2 – 2.5 c.	2 – 2.5 c.	2.5 – 3.5 c.	3.5 – 4.5 c.	3.5 – 4.5 c.
Vegetables	1.5 – 2 c.	2 – 2.5 c.	2.5 – 3 c.	2.5 – 3 c.	3 – 3.5 c.	3.5 – 4.5 c.	4.5 – 5 c.	4.5 – 5 c.
Grains	5 oz eq.	5-6 oz eq.	6-7 oz eq.	6-7 oz eq.	7-8 oz eq.	8-9 oz eq.	9-10 oz eq.	10-11 oz eq.
Dairy	2-3 c.	3 c.	3 c.	3 c.	3 c.	3 c.	3 c.	3 c.
Protein	4 oz eq.	5 oz eq.	5-5.5 oz eq.	5.5-6.5 oz eq.	6.5-7 oz eq.	7-7.5 oz eq.	7-7.5 oz eq.	7.5-8 oz eq.
Healthy Oils & Other Fats	4 tsp.	5 tsp.	5 tsp.	6 tsp.	6 tsp.	7 tsp.	8 tsp.	8 tsp.
Water & Super Beverages*	Women: 9 c. Men: 13 c.	Women: 9 c. Men: 13 c.	Women: 9 c. Men: 13 c.	Women: 9 c. Men: 13 c.	Women: 9 c. Men: 13 c.	Women: 9 c. Men: 13 c.	Women: 9 c. Men: 13 c.	Women: 9 c. Men: 13 c.

*May count up to 3 cups caffeinated tea or coffee toward goal

DAILY FOOD GROUP TRACKER

GROUP	FRUITS	VEGETABLES	GRAINS	PROTEIN	DAIRY	HEALTHY OILS & OTHER FATS	WATER & SUPER BEVERAGES
① Estimate Total							
② Estimate Total							
③ Estimate Total							
④ Estimate Total							
⑤ Estimate Total							
⑥ Estimate Total							
⑦ Estimate Total							

FOOD CHOICES   DAY ❶

Breakfast: _____
Lunch: _____
Dinner: _____
Snacks: _____

PHYSICAL ACTIVITY   steps/miles/minutes: _____   SPIRITUAL ACTIVITY

description: _____   description: _____

FOOD CHOICES — DAY 2
Breakfast: _____
Lunch: _____
Dinner: _____
Snacks: _____

PHYSICAL ACTIVITY steps/miles/minutes: _____
description: _____

SPIRITUAL ACTIVITY
description: _____

FOOD CHOICES — DAY 3
Breakfast: _____
Lunch: _____
Dinner: _____
Snacks: _____

PHYSICAL ACTIVITY steps/miles/minutes: _____
description: _____

SPIRITUAL ACTIVITY
description: _____

FOOD CHOICES — DAY 4
Breakfast: _____
Lunch: _____
Dinner: _____
Snacks: _____

PHYSICAL ACTIVITY steps/miles/minutes: _____
description: _____

SPIRITUAL ACTIVITY
description: _____

FOOD CHOICES — DAY 5
Breakfast: _____
Lunch: _____
Dinner: _____
Snacks: _____

PHYSICAL ACTIVITY steps/miles/minutes: _____
description: _____

SPIRITUAL ACTIVITY
description: _____

FOOD CHOICES — DAY 6
Breakfast: _____
Lunch: _____
Dinner: _____
Snacks: _____

PHYSICAL ACTIVITY steps/miles/minutes: _____
description: _____

SPIRITUAL ACTIVITY
description: _____

FOOD CHOICES — DAY 7
Breakfast: _____
Lunch: _____
Dinner: _____
Snacks: _____

PHYSICAL ACTIVITY steps/miles/minutes: _____
description: _____

SPIRITUAL ACTIVITY
description: _____

LIVE IT TRACKER

Name: _____

Date: _____ Week #: _____

My activity goal for next week:
○ None ○ <30 min/day ○ 30-60 min/day

loss/gain _____ Calorie Range: _____

My food goal for next week: _____
_____

My week at a glance:
○ Great ○ So-so ○ Not so great

Activity level:
○ None ○ <30 min/day ○ 30-60 min/day

RECOMMENDED DAILY AMOUNT OF FOOD FROM EACH GROUP

GROUP	DAILY CALORIES							
	1300-1400	1500-1600	1700-1800	1900-2000	2100-2200	2300-2400	2500-2600	2700-2800
Fruits	1.5 – 2 c.	1.5 – 2 c.	1.5 – 2 c.	2 – 2.5 c.	2 – 2.5 c.	2.5 – 3.5 c.	3.5 – 4.5 c.	3.5 – 4.5 c.
Vegetables	1.5 – 2 c.	2 – 2.5 c.	2.5 – 3 c.	2.5 – 3 c.	3 – 3.5 c.	3.5 – 4.5 c.	4.5 – 5 c.	4.5 – 5 c.
Grains	5 oz eq.	5-6 oz eq.	6-7 oz eq.	6-7 oz eq.	7-8 oz eq.	8-9 oz eq.	9-10 oz eq.	10-11 oz eq.
Dairy	2-3 c.	3 c.	3 c.	3 c.	3 c.	3 c.	3 c.	3 c.
Protein	4 oz eq.	5 oz eq.	5-5.5 oz eq.	5.5-6.5 oz eq.	6.5-7 oz eq.	7-7.5 oz eq.	7-7.5 oz eq.	7.5-8 oz eq.
Healthy Oils & Other Fats	4 tsp.	5 tsp.	5 tsp.	6 tsp.	6 tsp.	7 tsp.	8 tsp.	8 tsp.
Water & Super Beverages*	Women: 9 c. Men: 13 c.	Women: 9 c. Men: 13 c.	Women: 9 c. Men: 13 c.	Women: 9 c. Men: 13 c.	Women: 9 c. Men: 13 c.	Women: 9 c. Men: 13 c.	Women: 9 c. Men: 13 c.	Women: 9 c. Men: 13 c.

*May count up to 3 cups caffeinated tea or coffee toward goal

DAILY FOOD GROUP TRACKER

	GROUP	FRUITS	VEGETABLES	GRAINS	PROTEIN	DAIRY	HEALTHY OILS & OTHER FATS	WATER & SUPER BEVERAGES
1	Estimate Total							
2	Estimate Total							
3	Estimate Total							
4	Estimate Total							
5	Estimate Total							
6	Estimate Total							
7	Estimate Total							

FOOD CHOICES   DAY 1

Breakfast: _____
Lunch: _____
Dinner: _____
Snacks: _____

PHYSICAL ACTIVITY   steps/miles/minutes: _____
description: _____

SPIRITUAL ACTIVITY
description: _____

FOOD CHOICES — DAY 2
Breakfast: _____
Lunch: _____
Dinner: _____
Snacks: _____

PHYSICAL ACTIVITY — steps/miles/minutes: _____
description: _____

SPIRITUAL ACTIVITY
description: _____

FOOD CHOICES — DAY 3
Breakfast: _____
Lunch: _____
Dinner: _____
Snacks: _____

PHYSICAL ACTIVITY — steps/miles/minutes: _____
description: _____

SPIRITUAL ACTIVITY
description: _____

FOOD CHOICES — DAY 4
Breakfast: _____
Lunch: _____
Dinner: _____
Snacks: _____

PHYSICAL ACTIVITY — steps/miles/minutes: _____
description: _____

SPIRITUAL ACTIVITY
description: _____

FOOD CHOICES — DAY 5
Breakfast: _____
Lunch: _____
Dinner: _____
Snacks: _____

PHYSICAL ACTIVITY — steps/miles/minutes: _____
description: _____

SPIRITUAL ACTIVITY
description: _____

FOOD CHOICES — DAY 6
Breakfast: _____
Lunch: _____
Dinner: _____
Snacks: _____

PHYSICAL ACTIVITY — steps/miles/minutes: _____
description: _____

SPIRITUAL ACTIVITY
description: _____

FOOD CHOICES — DAY 7
Breakfast: _____
Lunch: _____
Dinner: _____
Snacks: _____

PHYSICAL ACTIVITY — steps/miles/minutes: _____
description: _____

SPIRITUAL ACTIVITY
description: _____

LIVE IT TRACKER

Name: _____

My activity goal for next week:
○ None ○ <30 min/day ○ 30-60 min/day

My food goal for next week: _____
_____

Date: _____ Week #: _____

loss/gain _____ Calorie Range: _____

My week at a glace:
○ Great ○ So-so ○ Not so great

Activity level:
○ None ○ <30 min/day ○ 30-60 min/day

RECOMMENDED DAILY AMOUNT OF FOOD FROM EACH GROUP

GROUP	DAILY CALORIES							
	1300-1400	1500-1600	1700-1800	1900-2000	2100-2200	2300-2400	2500-2600	2700-2800
Fruits	1.5 – 2 c.	1.5 – 2 c.	1.5 – 2 c.	2 – 2.5 c.	2 – 2.5 c.	2.5 – 3.5 c.	3.5 – 4.5 c.	3.5 – 4.5 c.
Vegetables	1.5 – 2 c.	2 – 2.5 c.	2.5 – 3 c.	2.5 – 3 c.	3 – 3.5 c.	3.5 – 4.5 c.	4.5 – 5 c.	4.5 – 5 c.
Grains	5 oz eq.	5-6 oz eq.	6-7 oz eq.	6-7 oz eq.	7-8 oz eq.	8-9 oz eq.	9-10 oz eq.	10-11 oz eq.
Dairy	2-3 c.	3 c.	3 c.	3 c.	3 c.	3 c.	3 c.	3 c.
Protein	4 oz eq.	5 oz eq.	5-5.5 oz eq.	5.5-6.5 oz eq.	6.5-7 oz eq.	7-7.5 oz eq.	7-7.5 oz eq.	7.5-8 oz eq.
Healthy Oils & Other Fats	4 tsp.	5 tsp.	5 tsp.	6 tsp.	6 tsp.	7 tsp.	8 tsp.	8 tsp.
Water & Super Beverages*	Women: 9 c. Men: 13 c.	Women: 9 c. Men: 13 c.	Women: 9 c. Men: 13 c.	Women: 9 c. Men: 13 c.	Women: 9 c. Men: 13 c.	Women: 9 c. Men: 13 c.	Women: 9 c. Men: 13 c.	Women: 9 c. Men: 13 c.

*May count up to 3 cups caffeinated tea or coffee toward goal

DAILY FOOD GROUP TRACKER

	GROUP	FRUITS	VEGETABLES	GRAINS	PROTEIN	DAIRY	HEALTHY OILS & OTHER FATS	WATER & SUPER BEVERAGES
1	Estimate Total							
2	Estimate Total							
3	Estimate Total							
4	Estimate Total							
5	Estimate Total							
6	Estimate Total							
7	Estimate Total							

FOOD CHOICES   DAY 1
Breakfast: _____
Lunch: _____
Dinner: _____
Snacks: _____

PHYSICAL ACTIVITY   steps/miles/minutes: _____
description: _____

SPIRITUAL ACTIVITY
description: _____

FOOD CHOICES — DAY 2
Breakfast: _____
Lunch: _____
Dinner: _____
Snacks: _____

PHYSICAL ACTIVITY   steps/miles/minutes: _____   **SPIRITUAL ACTIVITY**
description: _____   description: _____

FOOD CHOICES — DAY 3
Breakfast: _____
Lunch: _____
Dinner: _____
Snacks: _____

PHYSICAL ACTIVITY   steps/miles/minutes: _____   **SPIRITUAL ACTIVITY**
description: _____   description: _____

FOOD CHOICES — DAY 4
Breakfast: _____
Lunch: _____
Dinner: _____
Snacks: _____

PHYSICAL ACTIVITY   steps/miles/minutes: _____   **SPIRITUAL ACTIVITY**
description: _____   description: _____

FOOD CHOICES — DAY 5
Breakfast: _____
Lunch: _____
Dinner: _____
Snacks: _____

PHYSICAL ACTIVITY   steps/miles/minutes: _____   **SPIRITUAL ACTIVITY**
description: _____   description: _____

FOOD CHOICES — DAY 6
Breakfast: _____
Lunch: _____
Dinner: _____
Snacks: _____

PHYSICAL ACTIVITY   steps/miles/minutes: _____   **SPIRITUAL ACTIVITY**
description: _____   description: _____

FOOD CHOICES — DAY 7
Breakfast: _____
Lunch: _____
Dinner: _____
Snacks: _____

PHYSICAL ACTIVITY   steps/miles/minutes: _____   **SPIRITUAL ACTIVITY**
description: _____   description: _____

LIVE IT TRACKER

Name: _____

Date: _____ Week #: _____

My activity goal for next week:
○ None ○ <30 min/day ○ 30-60 min/day

loss/gain _____ Calorie Range: _____

My week at a glace:
○ Great ○ So-so ○ Not so great

My food goal for next week: _____

Activity level:
○ None ○ <30 min/day ○ 30-60 min/day

RECOMMENDED DAILY AMOUNT OF FOOD FROM EACH GROUP

GROUP	DAILY CALORIES							
	1300-1400	1500-1600	1700-1800	1900-2000	2100-2200	2300-2400	2500-2600	2700-2800
Fruits	1.5 – 2 c.	1.5 – 2 c.	1.5 – 2 c.	2 – 2.5 c.	2 – 2.5 c.	2.5 – 3.5 c.	3.5 – 4.5 c.	3.5 – 4.5 c.
Vegetables	1.5 – 2 c.	2 – 2.5 c.	2.5 – 3 c.	2.5 – 3 c.	3 – 3.5 c.	3.5 – 4.5 c.	4.5 – 5 c.	4.5 – 5 c.
Grains	5 oz eq.	5-6 oz eq.	6-7 oz eq.	6-7 oz eq.	7-8 oz eq.	8-9 oz eq.	9-10 oz eq.	10-11 oz eq.
Dairy	2-3 c.	3 c.	3 c.	3 c.	3 c.	3 c.	3 c.	3 c.
Protein	4 oz eq.	5 oz eq.	5-5.5 oz eq.	5.5-6.5 oz eq.	6.5-7 oz eq.	7-7.5 oz eq.	7-7.5 oz eq.	7.5-8 oz eq.
Healthy Oils & Other Fats	4 tsp.	5 tsp.	5 tsp.	6 tsp.	6 tsp.	7 tsp.	8 tsp.	8 tsp.
Water & Super Beverages*	Women: 9 c. Men: 13 c.	Women: 9 c. Men: 13 c.	Women: 9 c. Men: 13 c.	Women: 9 c. Men: 13 c.	Women: 9 c. Men: 13 c.	Women: 9 c. Men: 13 c.	Women: 9 c. Men: 13 c.	Women: 9 c. Men: 13 c.

*May count up to 3 cups caffeinated tea or coffee toward goal

DAILY FOOD GROUP TRACKER

	GROUP	FRUITS	VEGETABLES	GRAINS	PROTEIN	DAIRY	HEALTHY OILS & OTHER FATS	WATER & SUPER BEVERAGES
1	Estimate Total							
2	Estimate Total							
3	Estimate Total							
4	Estimate Total							
5	Estimate Total							
6	Estimate Total							
7	Estimate Total							

FOOD CHOICES   DAY 1

Breakfast: _____
Lunch: _____
Dinner: _____
Snacks: _____

PHYSICAL ACTIVITY   steps/miles/minutes: _____
description: _____

SPIRITUAL ACTIVITY
description: _____

FOOD CHOICES — DAY 2
Breakfast: _____
Lunch: _____
Dinner: _____
Snacks: _____

PHYSICAL ACTIVITY   steps/miles/minutes: _____
description: _____

SPIRITUAL ACTIVITY
description: _____

FOOD CHOICES — DAY 3
Breakfast: _____
Lunch: _____
Dinner: _____
Snacks: _____

PHYSICAL ACTIVITY   steps/miles/minutes: _____
description: _____

SPIRITUAL ACTIVITY
description: _____

FOOD CHOICES — DAY 4
Breakfast: _____
Lunch: _____
Dinner: _____
Snacks: _____

PHYSICAL ACTIVITY   steps/miles/minutes: _____
description: _____

SPIRITUAL ACTIVITY
description: _____

FOOD CHOICES — DAY 5
Breakfast: _____
Lunch: _____
Dinner: _____
Snacks: _____

PHYSICAL ACTIVITY   steps/miles/minutes: _____
description: _____

SPIRITUAL ACTIVITY
description: _____

FOOD CHOICES — DAY 6
Breakfast: _____
Lunch: _____
Dinner: _____
Snacks: _____

PHYSICAL ACTIVITY   steps/miles/minutes: _____
description: _____

SPIRITUAL ACTIVITY
description: _____

FOOD CHOICES — DAY 7
Breakfast: _____
Lunch: _____
Dinner: _____
Snacks: _____

PHYSICAL ACTIVITY   steps/miles/minutes: _____
description: _____

SPIRITUAL ACTIVITY
description: _____

LIVE IT TRACKER

Name: _____

My activity goal for next week:
○ None   ○ <30 min/day   ○ 30-60 min/day

My food goal for next week: _____
_____
_____

Date: _____ Week #: _____

loss /gain _____ Calorie Range: _____

My week at a glance:
○ Great   ○ So-so   ○ Not so great

Activity level:
○ None   ○ <30 min/day   ○ 30-60 min/day

RECOMMENDED DAILY AMOUNT OF FOOD FROM EACH GROUP

GROUP	DAILY CALORIES							
	1300-1400	1500-1600	1700-1800	1900-2000	2100-2200	2300-2400	2500-2600	2700-2800
Fruits	1.5 – 2 c.	1.5 – 2 c.	1.5 – 2 c.	2 – 2.5 c.	2 – 2.5 c.	2.5 – 3.5 c.	3.5 – 4.5 c.	3.5 – 4.5 c.
Vegetables	1.5 – 2 c.	2 – 2.5 c.	2.5 – 3 c.	2.5 – 3 c.	3 – 3.5 c.	3.5 – 4.5 c..	4.5 – 5 c.	4.5 – 5 c.
Grains	5 oz eq.	5-6 oz eq.	6-7 oz eq.	6-7 oz eq.	7-8 oz eq.	8-9 oz eq.	9-10 oz eq.	10-11 oz eq.
Dairy	2-3 c.	3 c.	3 c.	3 c.	3 c.	3 c.	3 c.	3 c.
Protein	4 oz eq.	5 oz eq.	5-5.5 oz eq.	5.5-6.5 oz eq.	6.5-7 oz eq.	7-7.5 oz eq.	7-7.5 oz eq.	7.5-8 oz eq.
Healthy Oils & Other Fats	4 tsp.	5 tsp.	5 tsp.	6 tsp.	6 tsp.	7 tsp.	8 tsp.	8 tsp.
Water & Super Beverages*	Women: 9 c. Men: 13 c.	Women: 9 c. Men: 13 c.	Women: 9 c. Men: 13 c.	Women: 9 c. Men: 13 c.	Women: 9 c. Men: 13 c.	Women: 9 c. Men: 13 c.	Women: 9 c. Men: 13 c.	Women: 9 c. Men: 13 c.

*May count up to 3 cups caffeinated tea or coffee toward goal

DAILY FOOD GROUP TRACKER

	GROUP	FRUITS	VEGETABLES	GRAINS	PROTEIN	DAIRY	HEALTHY OILS & OTHER FATS	WATER & SUPER BEVERAGES
1	Estimate Total							
2	Estimate Total							
3	Estimate Total							
4	Estimate Total							
5	Estimate Total							
6	Estimate Total							
7	Estimate Total							

FOOD CHOICES   DAY 1

Breakfast: _____
Lunch: _____
Dinner: _____
Snacks: _____

PHYSICAL ACTIVITY   steps/miles/minutes: _____
description: _____

SPIRITUAL ACTIVITY
description: _____

FOOD CHOICES — DAY 2

Breakfast: _____
Lunch: _____
Dinner: _____
Snacks: _____

PHYSICAL ACTIVITY   steps/miles/minutes: _____   **SPIRITUAL ACTIVITY**
description: _____   description: _____

FOOD CHOICES — DAY 3

Breakfast: _____
Lunch: _____
Dinner: _____
Snacks: _____

PHYSICAL ACTIVITY   steps/miles/minutes: _____   **SPIRITUAL ACTIVITY**
description: _____   description: _____

FOOD CHOICES — DAY 4

Breakfast: _____
Lunch: _____
Dinner: _____
Snacks: _____

PHYSICAL ACTIVITY   steps/miles/minutes: _____   **SPIRITUAL ACTIVITY**
description: _____   description: _____

FOOD CHOICES — DAY 5

Breakfast: _____
Lunch: _____
Dinner: _____
Snacks: _____

PHYSICAL ACTIVITY   steps/miles/minutes: _____   **SPIRITUAL ACTIVITY**
description: _____   description: _____

FOOD CHOICES — DAY 6

Breakfast: _____
Lunch: _____
Dinner: _____
Snacks: _____

PHYSICAL ACTIVITY   steps/miles/minutes: _____   **SPIRITUAL ACTIVITY**
description: _____   description: _____

FOOD CHOICES — DAY 7

Breakfast: _____
Lunch: _____
Dinner: _____
Snacks: _____

PHYSICAL ACTIVITY   steps/miles/minutes: _____   **SPIRITUAL ACTIVITY**
description: _____   description: _____

LIVE IT TRACKER

Name: _____   Date: _____ Week #: _____

My activity goal for next week:
○ None   ○ <30 min/day   ○ 30-60 min/day

loss /gain _____ Calorie Range: _____

My week at a glace:
○ Great   ○ So-so   ○ Not so great

My food goal for next week: _____
_____

Activity level:
○ None   ○ <30 min/day   ○ 30-60 min/day

RECOMMENDED DAILY AMOUNT OF FOOD FROM EACH GROUP

GROUP	DAILY CALORIES							
	1300-1400	1500-1600	1700-1800	1900-2000	2100-2200	2300-2400	2500-2600	2700-2800
Fruits	1.5 – 2 c.	1.5 – 2 c.	1.5 – 2 c.	2 – 2.5 c.	2 – 2.5 c.	2.5 – 3.5 c.	3.5 – 4.5 c.	3.5 – 4.5 c.
Vegetables	1.5 – 2 c.	2 – 2.5 c.	2.5 – 3 c.	2.5 – 3 c.	3 – 3.5 c.	3.5 – 4.5 c.	4.5 – 5 c.	4.5 – 5 c.
Grains	5 oz eq.	5-6 oz eq.	6-7 oz eq.	6-7 oz eq.	7-8 oz eq.	8-9 oz eq.	9-10 oz eq.	10-11 oz eq.
Dairy	2-3 c.	3 c.	3 c.	3 c.	3 c.	3 c.	3 c.	3 c.
Protein	4 oz eq.	5 oz eq.	5-5.5 oz eq.	5.5-6.5 oz eq.	6.5-7 oz eq.	7-7.5 oz eq.	7-7.5 oz eq.	7.5-8 oz eq.
Healthy Oils & Other Fats	4 tsp.	5 tsp.	5 tsp.	6 tsp.	6 tsp.	7 tsp.	8 tsp.	8 tsp.
Water & Super Beverages*	Women: 9 c. Men: 13 c.	Women: 9 c. Men: 13 c.	Women: 9 c. Men: 13 c.	Women: 9 c. Men: 13 c.	Women: 9 c. Men: 13 c.	Women: 9 c. Men: 13 c.	Women: 9 c. Men: 13 c.	Women: 9 c. Men: 13 c.

*May count up to 3 cups caffeinated tea or coffee toward goal

DAILY FOOD GROUP TRACKER

GROUP	FRUITS	VEGETABLES	GRAINS	PROTEIN	DAIRY	HEALTHY OILS & OTHER FATS	WATER & SUPER BEVERAGES
1 Estimate Total							
2 Estimate Total							
3 Estimate Total							
4 Estimate Total							
5 Estimate Total							
6 Estimate Total							
7 Estimate Total							

FOOD CHOICES   DAY 1

Breakfast: _____
Lunch: _____
Dinner: _____
Snacks: _____

PHYSICAL ACTIVITY   steps/miles/minutes: _____
description: _____

SPIRITUAL ACTIVITY
description: _____

FOOD CHOICES — DAY 2
Breakfast: _____
Lunch: _____
Dinner: _____
Snacks: _____

PHYSICAL ACTIVITY steps/miles/minutes: _____
description: _____

SPIRITUAL ACTIVITY
description: _____

FOOD CHOICES — DAY 3
Breakfast: _____
Lunch: _____
Dinner: _____
Snacks: _____

PHYSICAL ACTIVITY steps/miles/minutes: _____
description: _____

SPIRITUAL ACTIVITY
description: _____

FOOD CHOICES — DAY 4
Breakfast: _____
Lunch: _____
Dinner: _____
Snacks: _____

PHYSICAL ACTIVITY steps/miles/minutes: _____
description: _____

SPIRITUAL ACTIVITY
description: _____

FOOD CHOICES — DAY 5
Breakfast: _____
Lunch: _____
Dinner: _____
Snacks: _____

PHYSICAL ACTIVITY steps/miles/minutes: _____
description: _____

SPIRITUAL ACTIVITY
description: _____

FOOD CHOICES — DAY 6
Breakfast: _____
Lunch: _____
Dinner: _____
Snacks: _____

PHYSICAL ACTIVITY steps/miles/minutes: _____
description: _____

SPIRITUAL ACTIVITY
description: _____

FOOD CHOICES — DAY 7
Breakfast: _____
Lunch: _____
Dinner: _____
Snacks: _____

PHYSICAL ACTIVITY steps/miles/minutes: _____
description: _____

SPIRITUAL ACTIVITY
description: _____

WEEK 1 THE POWER OF THE MIND

WEEK 2 WHAT'S GOD LIKE?

WEEK 3 PRAYER: CONVERSING WITH GOD

WEEK 4 REFRAMING OBEDIENCE

WEEK 5 WHAT DOES GOD THINK ABOUT ME?

I sought the Lord, and he answered me; he delivered me from all my fears. Those who look to him are radiant; their faces are never covered with shame.

PSALM 34:4–5

But seek first his kingdom and his righteousness, and all these things will be given to you as well.

MATTHEW 6:33

I have told you these things, so that in me you may have peace. In this world you will have trouble. But take heart! I have overcome the world.

JOHN 16:33

Do nothing out of selfish ambition or vain conceit. Rather, in humility value others above yourselves, not looking to your own interests but each of you to the interests of the others.

PHILIPPIANS 2:3–4

And forgive us our debts, as we also have forgiven our debtors.

MATTHEW 6:12

WEEK 6 MOVING FROM FEAR TO FREEDOM

WEEK 7 KEEPING FIRST THINGS FIRST

WEEK 8 WHEN LIFE IS HARD

WEEK 9 IT'S NOT ALL ABOUT ME

WEEK 10 FORGIVENESS: WHAT IS, WHAT IT IS NOT

Love the Lord your God with all your heart and with all your soul and with all your mind and with all your strength.

MARK 12:30

No one is like you, O Lord; you are great, and your name is mighty in power. Who should not revere you, O King of the nations? This is your due.

JEREMIAH 10:6–7

Do not be anxious about anything, but in every situation, by prayer and petition, with thanksgiving, present your requests to God.

PHILIPPIANS 4:6

Observe what the Lord your God requires: Walk in obedience to him, and keep his decrees and commands, his laws and regulations, as written in the Law of Moses. Do this so that you may prosper in all you do and wherever you go. .

1 KINGS 2:3

How precious to me are your thoughts, God! How vast is the sum of them! Were I to count them, they would outnumber the grains of sand—when I awake, I am still with you.

PSALM 139:17–18